ABC GUIDE TO PSYCHOLOGICAL PER

ABC GUIDE
PSYCHOLOGICAL PERSPECTIVES
Level 3

Mark Walsh

ABC GUIDE TO PSYCHOLOGICAL PERSPECTIVES

textbook training

Published by Textbook Training *Publishers*
Learning support for health and social care

© Text copyright Mark Walsh 2016

Mark Walsh asserts the moral right to be identified as the author of this work.

All rights reserved.

Also available in this series:

Working in Health and Social Care – An ABC Guide for Students
ISBN 978 - 1533500151

Anatomy and Physiology – An ABC Guide for Students
ISBN 978 - 1533500182

Meeting Individual Care and Support Needs – An ABC Guide for Students
ISBN 978 - 1533500229

Psychological Perspectives – An ABC Guide for Students
ISBN 978 - 1533499790

Sociological Perspectives – An ABC Guide for Students
ISBN 978 - 1533500274

HEALTH AND SOCIAL CARE

Introduction

This *ABC Guide to Psychological Perspectives* covers 67 entries that define, discuss and explain a range of concepts, terms and theories that feature in human development units that are part of level 3 health and social care courses. These include the *Psychological Perspectives* units of the *BTEC National Level 3 Health and Social Care* and the *OCR Level 3 Cambridge Technical Health and Social Care* awards. It is also relevant to learners and tutors of *GCE AS / A2 Psychology* and Access courses. The *ABC Guide to Psychological Perspectives* has been written to provide learners with a broad ranging resource to support learning within these particular units.

Unlike a textbook, this book is not designed to be read sequentially. You can find and access information about any one entry as the need arises but also follow some links between entries to build up and develop your understanding of a topic area. Try using a particular term as a 'way in' or jumping off point and go from there! At the end of each entry the *See also* and *Health Connection* boxes are used to indicate how the term is connected to other issues, debates and topics within and beyond the unit you are studying. You are encouraged to follow up some of these links and to move between the entries to clarify and deepen your understanding. References are also provided where appropriate and could be followed up as a way of extending your knowledge and understanding if you have a strong interest in a particular topic or issue.

Active listening

Active listening involves actively focusing on and noticing what a person says or communicates both verbally and non-verbally. Psychologically, it is quite an involved and demanding skill to develop and use.

Active listening has become a core communication skill that all health and social care workers should develop. When you listen actively, you 'hear' a number of aspects of the other person's communication. As well as focusing on the words a person is speaking, paying attention to their body language and the paralinguistic aspects of their speech (volume, pitch, speed, tone) can tell the active listener something about the emotions behind them. Active listeners tend to be good at using minimal prompts to let the speaker know they are focusing, have heard and understood what is being communicated and would like to hear more.

Active listening relies on the care worker using behavioural and cognitive skills. The listener's behaviour is important as this must demonstrate they are paying attention whilst also encouraging the speaker to express themselves. Minimal prompts such as brief, subtle nods of the head, 'Mmm' sounds, affirming words like 'Yes' or very brief sentences like "Ok, go on' can be used to do this. Skilful active listeners use minimal prompts in an appropriate, timely way and resist over-using them in case the communication process becomes distorted or forced. At the same time as they are focusing on and using minimal prompts to encourage and support the speaker, an active listener has to also receive and make sense of the information and emotions being communicated.

This is where cognitive skills, particularly thinking and memory, play an important part.

The **humanistic perspective** provides good theoretical reasons for using active listening in a wide range of care settings and contexts. For example, active listening is an important means of putting the humanistic concepts of empathy, unconditional positive regard and respect for individuals into practice in all health and social care settings. Health and social care workers gradually develop and improve their listening and responding skills as they gain more experience. Becoming an active listener should be a goal that all health, social care and early years workers aspire to and use when interacting with and supporting others (Moss, 2015).

> The word
> LISTEN
> contains
> the same letters
> as the word
> SILENT.
>
> — Alfred Brendel

See also – Humanistic perspective; Empathy; Person-centred counselling
References – Moss, B. (2015), *Communication Skills in Health and Social Care*, Sage Publications

Addiction

An addiction involves the compulsive seeking of, and engagement with, 'reward' stimuli (e.g alcohol, gambling or sex) even though this has detrimental effects on a person's physical and/or mental health and social wellbeing.

In a health or social care context, a person who has a persistent, recurring compulsion to use a substance (alcohol, heroin, nicotine, for example) or to behave in a particular way (gambling, viewing pornography, playing computer games) that harms their health, wellbeing or relationships is said to have an addiction (Moss and Dyer, 2010). Some medical professionals will only give an addiction diagnosis if the person has a physical dependence on the substance and would experience physical withdrawal symptoms if they stopped using the substance they crave. However, other healthcare professionals, including some medical practitioners, accept that psychological dependence on a substance or activity is sufficient to diagnose addiction. A person who wishes to overcome an addiction will need to deal with the physical *and* psychological withdrawal symptoms that usually occur when they stop using an addictive substance or try to change their compulsive behaviour.

See also – Biological perspectives; Addiction therapy; Mental illness

References – A.C. Moss and K.R. Dyer (2010) *Psychology of Addictive Behaviour*, Palgrave Macmillan.

HEALTH AND SOCIAL CARE

Addiction therapy

An addiction therapy is a form of medical treatment and/or psychological therapy and support focused on enabling a person to recognise and overcome their addictive use of a harmful substance or to change a pattern of addictive behaviour.

Overcoming an addiction, particularly an addiction to drugs, involves dealing with both the physical and psychological aspects of a problematic and compulsive behaviour. Medical monitoring and treatment are generally effective and safe in helping people to deal with their physical dependencies and withdrawal symptoms. However, specialist addictions counselling and therapies may also be needed to help people overcome the powerful psychological compulsions, cravings and the mental and emotional dependencies that are often a part of addiction.

Various forms of psychological therapy are used to help people to recover from addiction. Typically, these include:

- *Cognitive behavioural therapy* – this teaches people to identify the moods, negative thoughts and situations that trigger their drug craving or addiction behaviour. The goal is to replace dysfunctional thinking and behaviour with positive thoughts and constructive, coping strategies.

- *Contingency management therapy* – this is typically used in residential addictions treatment to give people incentives (goods, vouchers, privileges) and rewards for abstaining from addiction behaviour. As such it is a form of behaviour modification (operant conditioning) and has the same strengths and weaknesses as this approach to psychological change.

- *Family / couples therapy* – this involves the partner, and sometimes the family members, of the person becoming part of the therapeutic process. This helps to keep the person engaged in therapy, can enable those closest to the person to be a force for change and also gives them an opportunity to deal with the distress and damage the person's addiction may have caused them.

- *Motivational interviewing* - the therapist works to understand and make positive use of the individuals wish to change and tackle their addiction. The person's motives, strengths and wish to change become the main focus of therapy not their 'problems'.

- *Maintenance therapy* – some people require long-term drug treatment and counselling / psychotherapy to manage their addiction and avoid relapsing. For example, some people addicted to heroin are prescribed methadone, a substitute drug, and have regular, ongoing therapy to prevent them relapsing and returning to heroin use.

HEALTH AND SOCIAL CARE

Group therapy is often used to treat addiction problems. A person is more likely to be challenged as well as supported within a group situation by others who have a deep insight into the experience and difficulties of addiction (and recovery from it). This can be used to make people face up to their addictive behaviour and the role they must play in their own recovery. Individual therapy tends to be used to treat addiction problems where they co-exist alongside another mental health problem. In these situations, the therapeutic approach is adapted to meet the individual's particular therapy and support needs.

See also – Cognitive behavioural therapy; Behaviour modification; Operant conditioning; Therapy/therapeutic

Anxiety

Anxiety refers to the feelings of unease, apprehension or fear that people experience in everyday life when they sense danger or believe something (or somebody) is a threat to them. Anxiety is a very common, normal and understandable human response that is not usually seen as a significant problem for most people most of the time.

In addition to being associated with particular ways of thinking and feeling, anxiety also has a biological basis. It is underpinned by the biochemical changes and musculoskeletal reactions that all human beings are 'programmed' with and which result in the flight/fight/freeze responses people have to sudden, acute threats. The physical symptoms of anxiety that accompany its psychological features are generally less severe but may still be unpleasant and distressing. They include headaches, nausea, trembling, fainting, tightness in the chest, tingling in the hands and feet, over-breathing and palpitations, for example.

Explaining anxiety

The nature and occurrence of anxiety can be explained in a number of ways, depending on which psychological perspective is adopted. For example, normal anxiety is seen as an 'adaptive' response to threat or danger by evolutionary and biological psychologists. They would argue that it enables people to avoid, protect or remove themselves from potentially dangerous or harmful situations. However, this doesn't explain how or why anxiety can become a problem for some people.

In practice, health and social care workers need to distinguish between normal anxiety and anxiety-based behaviour that is part of an illness-based condition or disorder.

Psychologists and care workers who adopt a psychodynamic perspective tend to see anxiety as the outcome or expression of deep, unconscious psychological processes. They would argue that anxiety is an everyday experience that most people manage effectively through the use of defence mechanisms. When a person's defence mechanisms fail or become ineffective, perhaps because the person has become too stressed for example, their anxieties leak out and are expressed in some form of psychological distress. By contrast, psychologists and care workers who adopt a cognitive behavioural therapy approach would see maladaptive learning and the reinforcement of anxiety-driven behaviour as the reason some people develop and struggle to overcome anxiety problems.

Anxiety disorders
It is thought that up to 10% of the UK population will experience an *anxiety disorder* at some point in their life (Royal College of Psychiatrists). 8.2 million people were diagnosed with an anxiety disorder in 2013 (Fineberg et al, 2013).

A person is said to have an anxiety disorder when their feelings of anxiety are prolonged, extreme or are too easily triggered in circumstances most people wouldn't see as anxiety-provoking. Medically defined anxiety disorders include generalised-anxiety disorder, social anxiety, post-traumatic stress disorder, panic disorder and phobias.

See also – Psychodynamic perspective; Defence mechanisms; Behaviour modification; Biofeedback; Post-traumatic Stress Disorder

Reference

Fineberg, N., Haddad, P., Carpenter, L., Gannon, B., Sharpe, R., Young, A., Joyce, E., Rowe, J., Wellsted, D., Nutt, D. and Sahakian, B. (2013). The size, burden and cost of disorders of the brain in the UK. *Journal of Psychopharmacology*, 27(9), pp.761-770.

HEALTH AND SOCIAL CARE

Applied Psychology

Applied psychology involves the use and application of psychological concepts, theories, methods and evidence to understand and solve real world problems.

Research and theory development within university-based academic psychology departments is now widely test and applied (put to work) in a broad range of occupational and everyday life situations (Ingleby 2010). For example, clinical, counselling and neuropsychology are all applied branches of the broader discipline of psychology that have clear health and social care applications. Additionally, many health and social care practitioners, including doctors, registered nurses, social workers and occupational therapists, for example, learn about and use elements of psychology in their specialist areas of health and social care practice. For example, psychological concepts and theories are widely used to understand and explain:

- Human behaviour, including health and illness behaviour
- Relationships, including personal, family and group r
- Learning and psychological development through the lifespan
- Learning difficulties, mental health problems and emotional disorders

See also – Behaviour; Biological perspectives; Psychological perspectives
References
Ingleby, E. (2010) *Applied Psychology for Social Work*, Learning Matters

Attitude change

An attitude is a disposition towards someone or something. Holding a particular attitude means that you have made a subjective evaluation or judgement about the person or thing in question. A person's attitudes involve their beliefs, thoughts and feelings and are expressed through their behaviour.

A person's attitudes are strongly influenced by their upbringing and socialisation but are never fixed or completely stable. We are constantly developing, reviewing and reshaping our attitudes in response to the interactions, communication and experiences we have with others in society. A broad range of social influences (the media, peers, co-workers, partners, family members etc) as well as the individual's own motivation to achieve cognitive consistency can lead a person to change or adjust their attitude.

Change your thoughts and you change your world.

Psychologists suggest that the following three psychological processes can all result in attitude change:

- *Compliance* – that is, people may change their attitude to comply with what they see as the expected way of behaving in a particular situation (Asch, 1956).
- *Identification* – that is, people may change their attitude in order to be more like someone they admire or like (a person they identify with).
- *Internalisation* – that is, a person's attitudes may change if they find that a new or different attitude or behaviour is more consistent with their internal and deeply-held values.

Festinger (1957) extended the study and understanding of attitude change by introducing the concept of 'cognitive dissonance' into psychology. This is the sense of unease or guilt people experience when they hold conflicting cognitions (thoughts / beliefs) or when there is an inconsistency between their attitude and their behaviour. Festinger argued that a person in this situation may be motivated to change their attitudes and beliefs in order to reduce the cognitive dissonance they are experiencing.

See also – Attitudes; Cognitive perspective;

References

Asch, S. E. (1956). 'Studies of independence and conformity: A minority of one against a unanimous majority'. *Psychological Monographs*, 70 (Whole no. 416).

Festinger, L. (1957) *A Theory of Cognitive Dissonance*, Stanford University Press.

Bandura's theory

Albert Bandura (b. 1925) is the Canadian psychologist responsible for developing some of the main principles of social learning theory.

Bandura recognized that behavioural psychology could only explain how people learn directly through experience. Bandura carried out experiments to show that people, and other animals, also learn *indirectly* by observing and imitating the behaviour of others. As a result, Bandura's social learning theory perspective focuses on the effects that other people, such as parents, teachers, friends, peer group members, celebrities, sports performers and pop stars, for example, can have on an individual's development and behaviour. In particular, Bandura's social learning theory argues that some behaviour is acquired or learnt through imitation of admired people or role models.

Bandura's famous 'Bobo Doll' experiment was used to develop and provide evidence for some of the principles of social learning theory. A bobo doll is a plastic inflatable toy that stands about 5 feet tall. It was usually painted with the face of a clown and was bottom-weighted to ensure that if it was hit, it would return to an upright position again.

Bandura et al's (1961) experimental study involved 36 boys and 36 girls, all 4 years of age. In the experiment, the children were divided into three groups (12 boys and 12 girls in each group) carefully matched for aggression levels. Children were allocated to one of three groups:

HEALTH AND SOCIAL CARE

1. An aggressive model group who saw an adult being physically and verbally abusive to a Bobo doll.
2. A non-aggressive model group who saw an adult act neutrally towards a Bobo doll.
3. A third control group didn't see an adult playing with the Bobo doll at all.

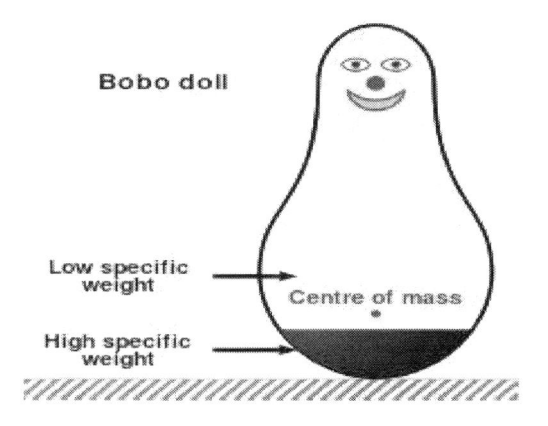

Figure 1 – An example of the type of Bobo doll used in Bandura's experiment.

All of the children spent time in a room with toys they weren't allowed to play with. They were then put in a room with a Bobo doll. Bandura et al (1961) found that the children who were part of the groups that saw an adult being verbally and physically aggressive towards the bobo doll were more likely to treat the doll aggressively themselves than those children who saw the bobo doll being treated well or didn't see an adult playing with the doll at all. Bandura's experiment showed that children don't just learn from the consequences of their own actions, but also model the behaviour of others.

Bandura (1961) argued that the bobo doll experiments showed that we learn through a process of imitating role models but that we only imitate those behaviour we see as being in our interests. Social learning theorists like Bandura say that for behaviour to be imitated it must be rewarded or reinforced in some way. This can occur through 'vicarious reinforcement' where an individual experiences indirect reinforcement by seeing their role model being reinforced. For example, a child may see their favourite footballer get away with a foul, score a goal and then get lots of praise from team mates and supporters. As a result, they may decide to copy this aspect of their admired role model's behaviour the next time they play football themselves.

The social learning theory approach suggests that learning, and the development of behaviour, sometimes occurs without the need for direct reinforcement. Admired people (role models) are able to influence an individual's behaviour and identity if the individual is motivated to be more like their role model. People are motivated to be more like their role models if they admire or desire the personal attributes or qualities associated with them.

See also – Role models; Reinforcement; Social learning theory

Reference
Bandura, A. Ross, D. and Ross, S.A. (1961), 'Transmission of aggression through imitation of aggressive models', *Journal of Abnormal and Social Psychology*, 63: 575-82

HEALTH AND SOCIAL CARE

Behaviour

Psychologists view behaviour as the observable responses a person makes, or the actions they take, in relation to specific stimuli.

In addition to investigating how learning can occur through stimulus-response associations (behavioural psychology), psychologists have also investigated and sought to explain the biological basis of human behaviour (biological psychology), the social influences on behaviour development (social learning theory) and the links between mental processes and behaviour (cognitive psychology). The development and expression of human behaviour remains a key focus of many contemporary psychologists who wish to understand connections between the human mind and how people respond and act in different situations.

Figure 2 – Human behaviour has developed in response to evolutionary and social influences.

See also – Behaviourism; Behaviour modification; Challenging behaviour; Conditioning

ABC GUIDE TO PSYCHOLOGICAL PERSPECTIVES

Behaviourism

Behaviourism is a major psychological perspective that focuses on human behaviour and learning processes. Behaviourism was the dominant perspective in psychology during the first half of the twentieth century. It continues to be widely used in health and social care settings, but is now less influential within mainstream psychology than it once was.

The behaviourist approach in psychology focuses on behaviour that can be observed. It is sometimes also known as 'learning theory' because its basic focus is on the way that human beings learn and the impact this has on their behaviour and relationships. For example, behaviourists believe that people have to learn how to make and maintain relationships and that the way we cope with stress and pressure is also the result of what we have learnt from others. Behaviourists claim that human behaviour is:

- learnt from experience
- more likely to be repeated if reinforcement occurs.

Reinforcement is the process by which a response is strengthened and thereby reinforced.

Ivan Pavlov (1849-1936), a Russian physiologist, and B.F Skinner (1904-1990), an American psychologist, are the theorists most closely associated with the behaviourist perspective. Pavlov inadvertently discovered the principles of classical conditioning whilst he was investigating digestion processes in dogs.

B.F. Skinner made a more deliberate attempt to investigate animal learning using rats and pigeons to test his theory of instrumental learning. The learning process that he identified and demonstrated is now known as operant conditioning.

The strengths and weaknesses or limitations of the behaviourist approach to psychology are summarized in the table below.

Strengths	Weaknesses / limitations
1. The behaviourist approach has been widely used to successfully modify (e.g phobias) and motivate (e.g weight loss) behaviour change.	1. Behaviourism reduces human behaviour to a simple stimulus-response level. This fails to take into account inner mental processes or wider cultural and environmental influences on behaviour.
2. Behavioural assessment and treatment is relatively quick, inexpensive and solution-focused.	2. Some care workers and psychologists are critical of behaviourism for being manipulative and for not addressing the underlying causes of an individual's problems.
3. Changes in behaviour can be easily measured, monitored and observed.	3. Behavioural treatments work well in controlled environments, especially with animals. They have a more limited application to the real-world behaviour of human beings.

See also – see Classical conditioning; Operant conditioning; Pavlov; Reinforcement; Behaviour modification

Behaviour modification

Behaviour modification is a behavioural psychology approach to changing human behaviour using rewards to reinforce new, desirable behaviours and/or extinguish unwanted or undesirable behaviour(s). It is based on operant conditioning principles.

Psychologists and care workers can use a variety of behavioural techniques to change unwanted, maladaptive and challenging behaviours and to stimulate and shape new forms of behaviour. Often the people who are given behavioural treatments use coping strategies that are damaging to themselves or others to deal with particular situations or stresses in life. Heavy drinking or drug-taking in response to stress or avoidance of travelling by aeroplane for fear of dying are examples of maladaptive behaviours.

The behavioural concepts of association and reinforcement can be used to trace back the origins of these kinds of behavioural and emotional problems and can help care practitioners understand an individual's behaviour.

Behaviour modification strategies

- **Aversion therapy** is a form of classical conditioning that uses negative reinforcement to change maladaptive behaviour. Negative reinforcement involves the removal of a discouraging or negative stimulus associated with a behaviour. It has been used as a treatment for alcoholism, for example, where the person is given a drug (Antabuse) that is perfectly safe and which has no side-effects – until the person drinks alcohol.

When alcohol is consumed, the person feels very unwell and may be violently sick. Over time the person learns to associate these unpleasant feelings and experiences with alcohol and stops drinking to avoid them. The same technique is used when a child's nails are painted with an unpleasant solution to deter them from biting them.

- **Systematic desensitisation** is a technique that is often used to treat phobias. This involves reducing and ultimately removing the power of a maladaptive association by gradually exposing the person to the thing they are frightened of (Wolpe, 1958). To do this the care practitioner and the phobic person first create a 'hierarchy of fear'. The treatment stage involves gradually exposing the person to varying degrees of fear whilst also helping them to relax and cope with each exposure. The goal is for the person to face the situation or object that they are fearful of or phobic about without worrying. Systematic desensitisation has been used effectively to help people overcome all kinds of phobias, from agoraphobia (fear of open spaces) to fear of spider, that cause distress and disrupt people's lives.

- **Token economy systems** are a behaviour modification strategy that use the principles of operant conditioning to stimulate or shape behaviours. Token economy systems use reinforcement (and to a lesser extent punishment) to change and shape an individual's behaviour. Typically, this involves establishing a system of 'token' rewards to reinforce desired behaviours. For example, parents and child care workers sometimes use 'reward' stickers to encourage young children to learn to use the potty and the toilet instead of a nappy. A token economy approach has been shown to be an effective way of controlling nigh-time bed-wetting in children capable of bladder control (Glazener and Evans, 2002).

Token economy systems were a common feature of mental health and learning disability services until the 1980s. They were generally used to motivate and reinforce the development of self-care skills (getting dressed, having a wash, taking part in activities) in unmotivated people who had lived in large institutions like mental hospitals for many years. Unfortunately, the 'token' would often be a cigarette or an actual token that people used to buy tobacco or cigarettes. In modern care settings, care practitioners are more likely to use social reinforcement in the form of verbal praise ('Well done, that's really great') to encourage desirable health behaviour and to build up the self-esteem and self-confidence of people who use the service.

Behaviour modification techniques are now widely used in early years and educational settings to shape and respond to children's behaviour. Many child care workers and teachers use 'reward' charts and positive forms of speech that socially reinforces desired behaviour or effort ('Well done', 'That's really good', 'Excellent work') in the classroom or care setting. You have probably experienced this approach in your own school or college career or through the approach your parents took to bringing you up.

See also – Behaviour; behaviourism; operant conditioning; Biofeedback
References
Glazener, C.M. and Evans, J.H. 2002), 'Simple behavioural and physical interventions for nocturnal enuresis in children', *Cochrane Database of Systematic Reviews*, 2: CD003637
Wolpe, J. (1958), *Psychotherapy by Reciprocal Inhibition*. Stanford, CA: Stanford University Press.

Biofeedback

Biofeedback is a treatment technique used to teach people to recognise and use signals from their body as a way of improving some aspect of their health, wellbeing or performance. It is based on the idea that there are strong connections between a person's biological functioning and their psychological experiences.

The person being taught to use biofeedback is usually attached to some form of device that detects physiological activity in a part of their body (muscle activity, breathing, brainwaves, skin temperature, for example). The person learns to use this information – often in conjunction with changes in their thinking, emotions and behaviour – to deliberately manipulate and control the physiological activity being monitored. This can lead to an improvement in their health, wellbeing or performance.

Over time many people learn to use the biofeedback technique they have learnt without the use of any equipment. Biofeedback has been used to treat people experiencing migraine, persistent headaches, anxiety problems, hyperhidrosis (excess sweating), bed-wetting, pain and stress. There is a significant mind-body connection in all of these health problems and typically no underlying physical disease or impairment that can be treated using conventional medical techniques such as medication or surgery.

Biofeedback is usually seen as a behavioural medicine technique though it can also be seen as a form of behaviour modification as the person is typically trying to change some aspect of their behaviour.

The effectiveness of biofeedback treatment is closely linked to whether the person is able to tune in to the way their body works and to develop relaxation and self-control skills.

See also – Behaviour; Behaviourism; Behaviour modification

HEALTH AND SOCIAL CARE

Biological perspective

The biological perspective in psychology applies the principles of biology to physiological, genetic and developmental aspects of human behaviour. The physiological strand of this approach focuses on nerves, neurotransmitters, brain circuits and basic biological processes, particularly maturation. A second strand of the biological perspective, known as evolutionary psychology, claims that many behaviours are deeply rooted in processes of natural selection. The claim is that those behavioural characteristics that are adaptive are passed on to the next generation through selective breeding. Those that aren't adaptive are not selected and disappear. As a result, users of this approach claim that to understand a particular type or example of human behaviour, we need to identify what natural selection designed it to do. Because biological psychologists are interested in the interconnection of mental and physiological processes, they tend to focus on:

- sensation and perception
- motivated behaviour (hunger, thirst, sex)
- movement control
- learning and memory
- emotion
- sleep and biological rhythms
- reasoning and decision-making

Some of the key principles on which biological psychology is based include:

1. there are biological correlates of behaviour e.g neurotransmitters, hormones, genes, specialised brain areas, body control systems.
2. animal research can provide insight into human behaviour i.e non-human and human biological processes are the same.
3. human behaviour is, at least partly, and perhaps largely, genetically-based. Genetic inheritance is seen to predispose if not quite determine some behaviours. This is supported in twin study evidence.

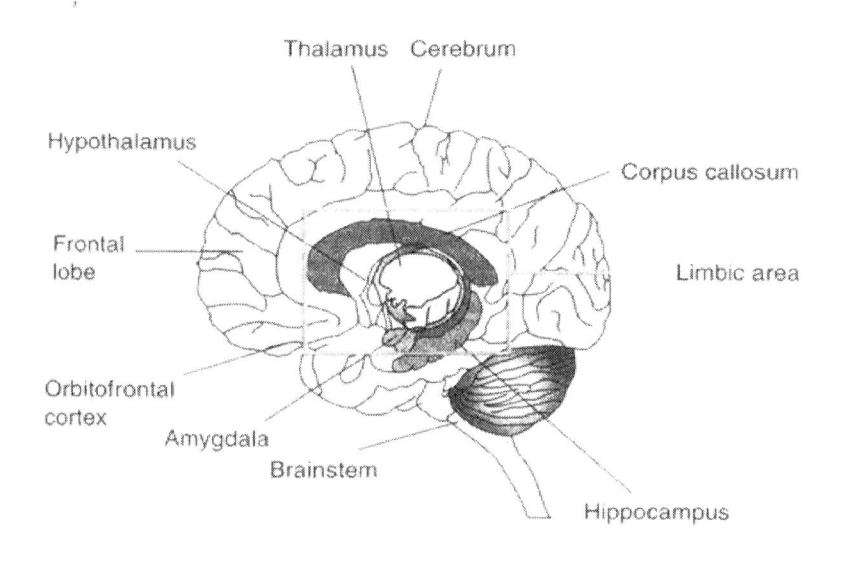

Figure 3 – Key features of the human brain

Biological psychology emerged as a powerful scientific perspective in the 1980's as scientific and technological developments provided greater insight into the way the brain and human biological processes worked. New brain and body scanning techniques and developments in genetics played a key part in this. Biological approaches remain very important in psychology today, particularly in the form of cognitive neuroscience. This brings together the biological and cognitive perspectives to investigate and explain the brain-based aspects of human psychology.

See also – Maturational theory; Genetic influences; Nervous system; Endocrine system; Developmental norms; Biofeedback

Challenging behaviour

Challenging behaviour is any form of behaviour that is out of keeping with the expected standards or patterns of behaviour in a culture or society. In effect, it 'challenges' normal expectations and standards.

It may be the intensity, frequency or duration of the behaviour that is unusual and which puts the person or other people at risk that makes a person's behaviour 'challenging'. Challenging behaviour is usually associated with adults who have learning disabilities, mental health problems or dementia and with children experiencing 'tantrums'. Self-harm, violence, inappropriate sexual behaviour, selective incontinence and vandalism are all common types of challenging behaviour.

Behavioural analysis and treatment of challenging behaviour typically tries to identify the causes, triggers and consequences of the behaviour. Operant conditioning principles are then used to help the person develop new, more socially acceptable ways of behaving. Where a person's challenging behaviour is more self-destructive or self-defeating (drug or alcohol misuse, for example) and they are capable of developing insight into it, psychodynamic therapy may be used to expose, explore and deal with unconscious motives and influences underpinning the pattern of behaviour.

See also – Behaviourism; Behaviour modification; Operant conditioning; Psychodynamic perspective

HEALTH AND SOCIAL CARE

Child abuse

Child abuse occurs when a child is subjected to physical, emotional or psychological harm, sexual molestation or neglect.

Childhood abuse could involve:

- physical abuse where injuries are deliberately inflicted or a health problem is caused by neglect.
- emotional abuse such as persistent criticism, manipulation or devaluing of the child, making unrealistic demands on or having impossibly high expectations of a child.
- sexual abuse where children view or are made to watch sexual acts, are exposed to pornography, are molested (touched sexually) or are encouraged or forced to take part in sexual acts (including intercourse and oral sex).

Detection of childhood abuse is difficult even though the impact on the child is often severe and long-lasting. It often requires inter-agency collaboration between health and social care practitioners, education staff and the police, for example. In addition, the willingness of the child, a non-abusing parent or somebody else close to the child is often needed to alert child protection professionals or school staff to suspected or actual abuse or neglect.

See also – Early experiences

Classical conditioning

Classical conditioning is a basic, associative learning process that occurs when two stimuli are repeatedly paired. A response that is naturally produced by the first stimuli is eventually elicited by the second, non-naturally occurring stimuli alone.

Ivan Pavlov (1849 – 1936) first illustrated the process and principles of classical conditioning. In Pavlov's experiments a dog was attached to a harness and to monitors that measured the rate at which it salivated. Pavlov thought that he could learn more about digestion in dogs if he measured the amount of saliva they produced when food was presented to them. However, Pavlov noticed that the dogs used in his experiment didn't have to taste or smell any food to begin salivating. They would salivate as soon as they realised food was being brought to them. For example, the dogs would begin salivating when they heard the footsteps of the approaching experimenter or laboratory assistant. This intrigued Pavlov because the belief at the time was that dogs and other animals salivated as a reflex response to food touching their tongue. Pavlov wondered instead whether the dogs were salivating because they had somehow learnt to associate food with the sound of the experimenter's steps, and that they were salivating in anticipation of the food. Pavlov worked out what was happening and in the process also identified the main principles of associative learning or classical conditioning.

HEALTH AND SOCIAL CARE

Classical conditioning explained

Food makes a dog salivate automatically – they don't have to think about it or learn to salivate when presented with food. In behavioural terms, this is known as an unconditioned response (UR). The food causing salivation is known as an unconditioned stimulus (US).

Pavlov's experiment involved presenting a dog with food whilst he rang a bell. The aim was to see if the dog would learn to associate the bell with food. Pavlov found that repeated trials of this pairing (bell plus food) led the dog to associate the bell with food. In fact, after a short while the dog would salivate simply when the bell was rung (and no food was presented). Pavlov explained this by saying that the dog had developed or learned a conditioned response (CR) of salivation in response to the conditioned stimulus (CS) of the bell.

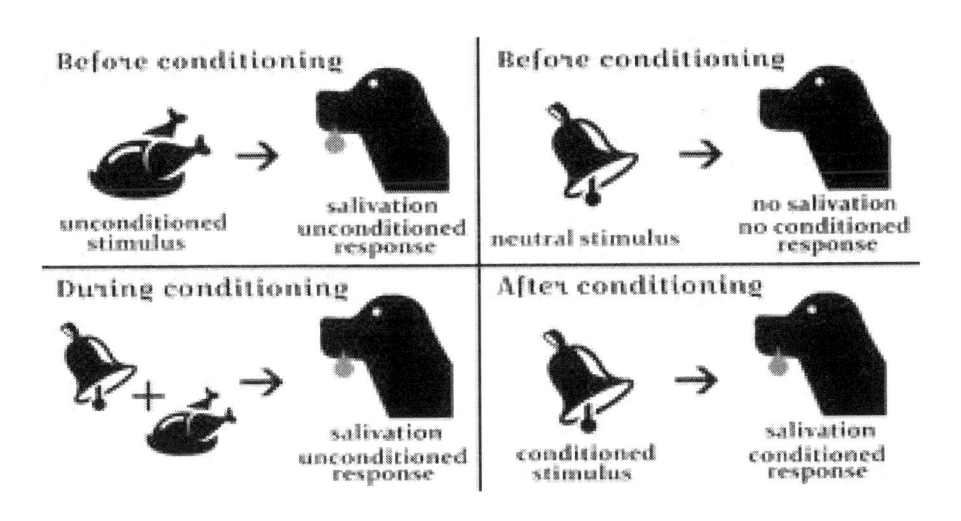

Figure 4 – Pavolv's classical conditioning experiment explained.

ABC GUIDE TO PSYCHOLOGICAL PERSPECTIVES

In simple terms, Pavlov's experiment demonstrates that animal's partly acquire their behaviour through conditioning processes (learning). Human are animals too, so the principles of associative learning also apply to us! For example, road vehicle drivers have (usually) been conditioned to put their foot on the brake when they see a red traffic light.

See also – Pavlov, Ivan; Behaviourism; Conditioning; Operant conditioning; Reinforcement

HEALTH AND SOCIAL CARE

Cognitive behavioural therapy

Cognitive behaviour therapy is a form of talking therapy that helps people to change the way they think and behave as a way of managing their problems. It is based on the premise that cognition (acquiring knowledge and forming beliefs) has a direct influence on a person's mood and behaviour.

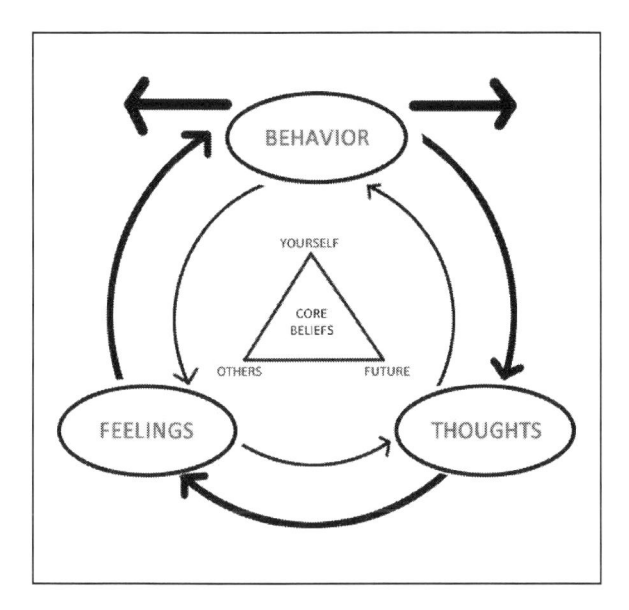

Figure 5 – Beck's cognitive triad

Cognitive behaviour therapy (CBT) was developed by Aaron T. Beck (1967) to treat depression. Beck identified a 'cognitive triad' (see diagram above) based on a negative self-appraisal that leads to negative beliefs about the world and the future – the individual sees themselves as powerless to overcome their difficulties.

The aim of CBT is to challenge negative thoughts and to enable each person to develop an alternative, positive view of the world. A 'thought diary' may be used to collect or catch 'negative automatic thoughts' and patterns of negative thinking. The care practitioner and client can then work out ways of challenging them. A key strategy is to consider the evidence for the negative thoughts and what the alternatives might be.

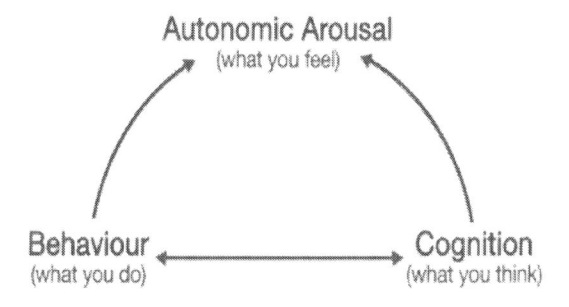

```
            Autonomic Arousal
              (what you feel)

      ↗                      ↖
    /                            \
  /                                \
Behaviour  ←——————————→  Cognition
(what you do)              (what you think)
```

Figure 6 – The ABC of CBT theory

Cognitive behavioural therapy is widely used in UK health and social care services. It is an effective treatment for anxiety and depression and is often available within primary care and mental health services. In practice, CBT is a short-term, easy to engage with and evidence-based form of mental health treatment that can be delivered by a range of health and social care workers who have received additional training. It also has the advantage of turning a person from a 'patient' into their own therapist. This is because, once they have learnt some new coping strategies, CBT enables the individual to identify and deal with their own thinking errors.

See also – Cognitive perspective; Depression; Anxiety; Phobia; Mental illness; Post-traumatic stress disorder; Behaviour; Challenging behaviour

References

Beck, A.T. (1967). *The diagnosis and management of depression.* Philadelphia, PA: University of Pennsylvania Press.

Cognitive perspective

The cognitive perspective is one of the main approaches used within contemporary academic and applied psychology to investigate and explain key aspects of human psychological functioning. The cognitive approach is distinctive in the way that it sees human beings as information-processors and compares human mental processes to software running on a computer (the brain).

Cognitive Psychology

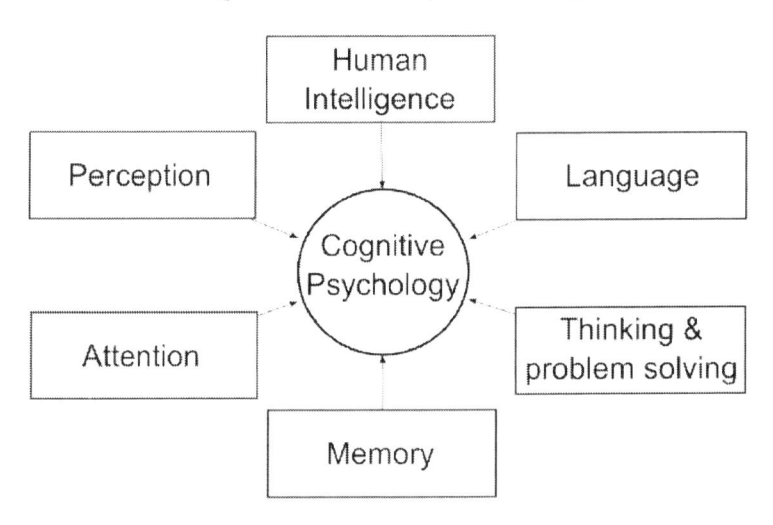

Figure 7 – Key issues in cognitive psychology

The cognitive perspective rose to prominence in the late 1950's when it started to challenge the narrow focus that behaviourism had on observable behaviour. Cognitive psychologists believed that internal mental processes should also be studied alongside behaviour.

Psychologists and care workers using this perspective now typically study or work with people experiencing perceptual, memory, language and intellectual development or thinking problems. That is, aspects of cognition (mental activity), or the way the brain works.

Many contemporary psychologists would describe themselves as cognitive psychologists. The cognitive approach, and the view that mental events are characterised by an information-flow that has to be dealt with, is very popular in health and social care settings too. Specialist counsellors and therapists using forms of cognitive therapy, doctors, nurses and other health care practitioners and social care workers also incorporate cognitive techniques into their relationship-building and intervention strategies. All draw on the 'cognitive triad' concept that links thinking, emotion and behaviour but also recognises that the brain's ability to process information is central to this.

Strengths	Weaknesses / limitations
1. Recognises that influences on human behaviour are broader and more complex than simple stimulus-response factors.	1. Ignores the role of biology, emotions, consciousness and free will in human learning and behaviour.
2. Shows how mental processes and the brain play a key part in the way people learn and behave.	2. Doesn't recognise the role of the unconscious and early experiences in understanding an individual's behaviour.

3. Sees the person as making some active choices (through creating meaning, memory, decision-making and use of judgement) in what they learn and how they behave.	3. Ignores the human experience of emotions and the powerful ways they can affect learning, behaviour and development.
4. CBT is based on a scientific, evidence-based approach to psychological treatment.	4. CBT is criticised for treating a person's symptoms rather than the causes of their problems.
5. The cognitive approach can be applied quite widely in the health and social care field.	5. It is reductionist and deterministic, suggesting that complex human psychological processes and experiences can be explained largely in terms of brain functioning.

See also – Cognitive Behavioural Therapy; Jean Piaget; Learning difficulties; Depression; Post-traumatic stress disorder; Personal constructs

HEALTH AND SOCIAL CARE

Conditioning

Conditioning is a behavioural term that is used to describe human and animal learning processes. There are two types of behavioural conditioning:

- classical conditioning - learning to make an association between two events (Pavlov).
- operant conditioning - the use of consequences to influence the occurrence of particular behaviours (Skinner).

Conditioning is a key feature of behaviourism and social learning theory and is the basis of behaviour modification techniques and treatments.

See also – Behaviourism; Behaviour modification; Classical conditioning; Operant conditioning; Reinforcement; Pavlov; Skinner

Culture

The concept of culture refers to the common values, beliefs and customs or way of life of a group, or sub-group, of people within a particular society or part of society.

Culture may affect physical growth and development where cultural beliefs or practices influence food choices, patterns of exercise and use of health care services, for example. Social development may also be affected by culture where cultural beliefs or practices influence attitudes, values and opportunities to develop and experience friendships and other non-family relationships. Emotional development may also be affected by extended family structures, by the closeness or expected pattern of relationships within the family and by a person's identification with their cultural heritage. In these different ways, culture can play a very important, though often unseen, role in shaping our personal growth and development.

It is also important to note that the psychological approaches and theories we use – our ways of understanding and explaining psychological development – may not be universally applicable. Cross-cultural variations exist in the way people develop and experience themselves and the world psychologically. It is important that care workers are not culturally 'blind' to the influence a person's cultural background may have on their behaviour and way of relating to others.

See also – Depression; Mental illness; Cognitive Behavioural Therapy

HEALTH AND SOCIAL CARE

Defence mechanisms

In psychodynamic theory, defence mechanisms are coping strategies designed to reduce anxiety that arises from unacceptable or harmful impulses deep in the unconscious.

Psychodynamic psychologists argue that people often use defence mechanisms to try to control their anxieties without being aware that they are doing so. Their anxieties may then manifest themselves in physical symptoms and illnesses, challenging behaviour or emotional distress. This can be very difficult for the individuals concerned and health care staff to deal with - the person has some physical symptoms or problems but there is no obvious physical, medical or other cause. In circumstances like these, particularly where the symptoms have been long lasting, a psychodynamic approach can be helpful in revealing the psychological root causes of the person's problems and also provides a way of addressing them.

Within the psychodynamic perspective, defence mechanisms are a way of protecting the ego from distress. They allow us to unconsciously block out experiences that overwhelm us. Table 1 describes a range of examples of defence mechanisms.

ABC GUIDE TO PSYCHOLOGICAL PERSPECTIVES

Figure 8 - Examples of ego defence mechanisms

Defence mechanism	Effect	Example
Repression	Person forgets an event or experience.	No recollection of a serious car crash.
Regression	Revert to an earlier stage of development.	Bedwetting when sibling is born or school begins.
Denial	Pushing events or emotion out of consciousness.	Refusal to accept you have a substance misuse problem.
Projection	Personal faults or negative feelings are attributed to someone else.	Accusing a colleague of being angry or thoughtless when you are really feeling this way.
Displacement	Redirecting desire or other strong emotions onto another person.	Shouting at your partner instead of at yourself or your best friend.

See also – Freud; psychoanalysis; Psychodynamic perspective; Unconscious mind

HEALTH AND SOCIAL CARE

Depression

Depression is a biomedical (psychiatric) diagnosis characterised by a combination of emotional (sadness, loss of pleasure, guilt), cognitive (negative self-beliefs, poor concentration) and physical (sleep and appetite disturbance, fatigue) symptoms. Most people living in Western societies recognise 'depression' as a low or flat mood and link it to mental health problems. The term 'depression' has also become a popular way of describing the experience of 'sadness'. However, whilst the experience of sadness is universal, it's description (and diagnosis) as 'depression' varies across cultures.

According to some critical psychiatrists, Western societies have medicalised sadness, calling it 'depression' (Horwitz and Wakefield, 2007) to justify using an illness-based approach to understanding and explaining it. It is seen as the 'common cold' of Western psychiatry, that is, a very common condition that is widely diagnosed. Some medical and mental health practitioners treat it as a mood disturbance, downplaying the cognitive aspects of negative thinking and the somatic or physical symptoms (poor appetite, poor sleep etc) that are often part of the condition. In fact, psychiatrists tend not to have a strong, shared agreement about what depression is though it is more than feeling upset or a bit low in mood.

People who are diagnosed with depression generally experience feelings of hopelessness, sadness, tearfulness and intense anxiety as well as a number of physical symptoms.

Sometimes it is possible to link a person's depression to an event or experience (e.g bereavement or other significant loss) that would have an understandably negative effect on most people. This is sometimes referred to as a reactive depression. However, when a person's depression is prolonged, extreme or without obvious cause, the person may be diagnosed as clinically depressed and be given a mental illness diagnosis.

Figure 9 - Symptoms of depression

Psychological symptoms	Physical symptoms
Lack of motivation Low self-esteem Despair Hopelessness Worthlessness Guilt	Disturbed sleep Poor appetite or over-eating Slowed speech Slowed movement Gastric problems Fatigue / low energy Bodily pain

10 – 15% of the population experience the symptoms of depression at any point in time. It is often experienced by people who also experience other social inequalities (poverty, discrimination, unemployment, etc).

See also – Anxiety; Biological psychology; Cognitive Behavioural Therapy; Mental illness; Culture
Reference:
A.V. Horwitz and J.C. Wakefield (2007), *The Loss of Sadness: How Psychiatry Transformed Normal Sadness into Depressive Disorder*, Oxford University Press

HEALTH AND SOCIAL CARE

Developmental norms

Developmental norms are the milestones or stages of physical, emotional or cognitive development that human beings are expected to achieve or follow at particular ages.

Human growth and development follows a fairly predictable pattern. Observation, experience and research have shown that specific patterns of growth and development tend to occur within particular time periods. Growth and developmental changes also tend to occur in a particular sequence. For example, when a baby can sit up unaided, it will develop the ability to crawl, followed by the ability to stand up and then the ability to walk. A 'developmental norm' is created by linking this sequence of expected growth and development to an expected timeframe. Knowledge of developmental norms provide a useful guide for assessing an infant's or a child's pattern of growth and development.

A skilled, knowledgeable practitioner would be able to use their understanding of developmental norms to identify whether an individual's development at specific points was age-appropriate. They would also be able to identify developmental delay and problems. Various cognitive and social skills are assessed as well as physical and motor abilities.

The value of developmental norms is that they can provide health and social care workers with hard data (based on scientific theory and observation) about an individual's development relative to that of others. Identification of developmental problems can then quickly lead to treatment or other interventions to support the child or young person.

It is important to note that the times at which different individuals achieve the same developmental norms may vary. It is not correct to say an infant, child or adolescent is 'abnormal' if he or she reaches a developmental norm at a slightly different time from the expected pattern. There may be a number of reasons for advanced and delayed development, none of which make the individuals development 'abnormal'

See also – Genetics; Maturational theory; Nature versus Nurture debate

HEALTH AND SOCIAL CARE

Early experiences

The term 'early experiences' is typically applied to children under five years of age (in early childhood) as this is often seen as a key developmental period in psychological literature. There is, in fact, a vast research literature on the developmental importance of an individual's early years. The basic assumption is that a person's early relationships and experiences have a profound effect, and ongoing impact, on their cognitive, social and emotional development throughout their life.

The very early years of life are seen as important to children's development as well as for later adult wellbeing. In particular, attachment relationships, parenting-style and the material and environmental circumstances of a person's early years have been shown to affect educational attainment in childhood and adolescence as well as emotional wellbeing later in life. Early experiences of poverty, abuse and neglect can have a profound impact on development because of the way a child's natural, innate abilities and vulnerabilities can be negatively influenced and damaged by these external, environmental factors.

Government investment in early years services and facilities is a response to this and is seen as beneficial to learning and development because of the way that positive early experiences and support can prevent problems and difficulties developing in later life.

Psychodynamically, a person's early childhood experiences is seen to play a crucial part in their later development. For example, traumatic and confusing events that have been repressed or pushed into the unconscious are thought to 'leak out' in dreams, irrational behaviour and in psychological distress because the emotional pain linked to them has not been dealt with.

See also – Child abuse; Psychodynamic perspective; Freud; Parenting style; Separation (and loss)

HEALTH AND SOCIAL CARE

Eating disorders

An eating disorder involves an abnormal attitude towards food that may lead to eating excessively and then vomiting (bulimia nervosa), food avoidance (anorexia nervosa) behaviour or overeating large amounts of food in a short time period (binge eating disorder).

Eating disorders tend to emerge in adolescence and are much more likely to be experienced by girls and women rather than boys and men. They are often motivated (and maintained) by a fear of weight gain and of the body developing into a mature adult size and shape, though these are not the only psychological reasons for eating disorders. Experiences of abuse, family dysfunction and relationship breakdown, loss and grief as well as difficulties adjusting to and accepting physical, emotional and social change during puberty have all been linked to the onset of eating disorders.

People who experience eating disorders may engage in excessive amounts of exercise, use laxatives and self-induce vomiting to purge themselves of food. Many people who experience eating disorders manage and deal with their problems without professional help. Where a person's weight loss becomes dangerous or they acknowledge the need for help and support, treatment can be provided by primary care or specialist mental health services, depending on the nature and severity of the person's difficulties.

See also – Mental illness; Anxiety; Depression; Self-concept; Self-image; Self-esteem; Self-harm

Empathy

The concept of empathy refers to the ability to experience the feelings of another person, from the other person's perspective.

Empathy involves active listening, is often quite difficult to do and is distinct from sympathy. It does not involve making any guesses or assumptions about what the other person is *really* thinking or feeling. In fact, the listener needs to put aside any preconceptions they have in order to recognise how the person is struggling to deal with specific problems. Tschudin (1982) uses the metaphor of helping a man stuck in a ditch to illustrate the difference between empathy and sympathy:

"The sympathetic helper goes and lies in the ditch with him and bewails the situation with him. The unsympathetic helper stands on the bank and shouts 'come on, get yourself out of that ditch!' The empathic helper climbs down to the victim but keeps one foot on the bank and is thus able to help the victim out of the trouble on to firm ground again."

The humanistic concept of empathy is now widely accepted as an important part of care relationships and health and social care practice generally. Health and social care workers can make their interactions with service users, family members and colleagues more effective by using empathy appropriately, gaining insight into the needs and experience of service users in an alert, calm way, without having to actually experience it directly.

HEALTH AND SOCIAL CARE

Using empathy also gives health and social care workers a way of communicating with the real person behind the label of service user, relative or colleague.

See also – Humanistic perspective; Person-centred counselling; Rogers, Carl

References

V. Tschudin (1982) *Counselling skills for Nurses*, Bailliere Tindall.

Endocrine system

The endocrine system consists of a collection of glands that secrete hormones directly into the circulatory system. Their role is to influence the metabolic activity of cells.

The endocrine system consists of the:
- Pituitary gland
- Thyroid gland
- Parathyroid gland
- Adrenal gland
- Pineal gland
- Thymus gland

The hormones released by these glands travel in the blood to target cells. This then triggers an effect in the body such as:

- growth and development
- metabolism
- reproduction / menstrual cycle
- energy balance
- fluid and electrolyte balance
- responses to stress and danger

In effect, the hormones released by the endocrine system control and affect many body functions and organs, as well as behaviour. In addition, the brain and endocrine system are able to communicate with each other via the hypothalamus. This part of the brain is central to homeostasis and receives information on the internal state of the body.

HEALTH AND SOCIAL CARE

It also sends information to the autonomic nervous system and to the pituitary gland immediately underneath it.

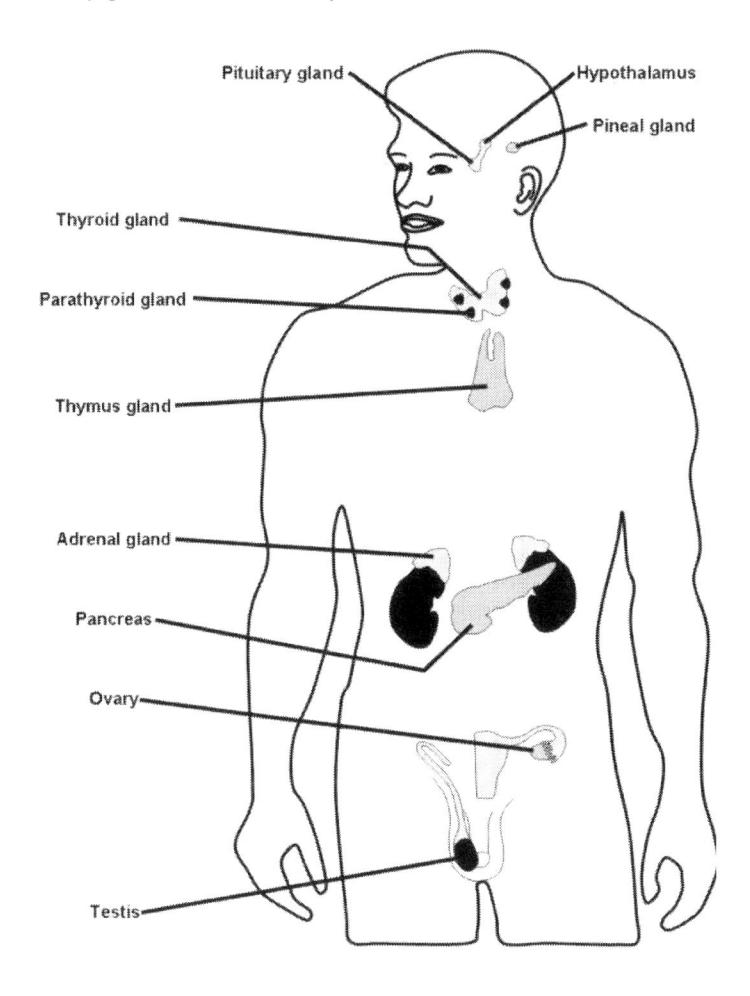

Figure 10 – Location of endocrine glands in the human body

The release of hormones from a person's endocrine glands can have a powerful effect on their behaviour and how they feel. Melatonin, released from the pineal glands, acts on the brain stem to synchronize an individual's pattern of sleep and activity, for example. The pineal gland responds to the external environment by releasing more melatonin as daylight fades, helping the person to go to sleep. Melatonin production is reduced as daylight returns. Similarly, you are probably aware of the link between testosterone and a person's level of aggression. The release of testosterone into the blood is linked to an increase in aggressiveness.

See also – Stress (and coping)

HEALTH AND SOCIAL CARE

Ethics

Ethics are moral principles that guide thinking and behaviour.

One way of explaining ethics is to see them as principles linked to a fundamental sense of 'right' and 'wrong' that guide personal and professional behaviour. The ethical standards and values that we accept and adopt guide the way that we think about and respond to others. As well as providing guidance on how to behave (such as to 'protect confidentiality' or 'accept diversity'), ethics point us towards morally acceptable ways of behaving and relating to others. Ethics tell us how we ought to behave and provide us with benchmarks or norms against which to assess our own and other peoples' attitudes, decisions and behaviour.

In health and social care contexts, ethical principles are embedded in and expressed through the codes of practice and codes of conduct that must be followed by registered practitioners. Ethical codes are used to regulate and guide the behaviour and approaches used by these care practitioners in their everyday work. This is important because ethical issues tend to be integral to, or part of, the care-related decision-making faced by a health and social care worker rather than something to be addressed separately. Typically, these codes, and ethical principles generally, become important when a practitioner has to make a decision about what action(s) are right and wrong in particular circumstances.

See also – Therapy/ therapeutic; Psychological interventions

ABC GUIDE TO PSYCHOLOGICAL PERSPECTIVES

Family therapy

Family Therapy involves a range of techniques and strategies that aim to help families deal with relationship problems and to function more effectively and harmoniously. It is a particular type of group therapy and is unusual in UK health and social care settings where individual (one-to-one) and group therapies delivered to groups of unrelated individuals are far more common.

A number of different types, or forms, of family therapy exist. Most are based on the idea that rigid rules and repeating patterns of behaviour within a family can be destructive. For example, blaming, scapegoating, shouting at, physical abuse or the isolation or withdrawal of particular family members may be a feature of a poorly functioning family. These types of negative behaviour may be seen by the family therapist as a way in which the family 'solves' the internal difficulties they have but are ultimately destructive to the individuals who experience them and to the family as a whole.

Figure 11 – Family therapy sessions treat the family as a communication system

The systems approach to family therapy is widely used and is an influential way of understanding and addressing problems within families. It suggests that family relations and the behaviours of individuals within the family are part of a 'system'. The implications of this are that the way each person behaves affects the behaviour of others. Consequently, because all behaviours are linked within a family, the pattern of behaviour and relationships must be considered as a whole.

Simply identifying and trying to treat the 'problem behaviours' of one or two individuals will not solve broader family dysfunction. The role of the family therapist is to offer an 'outside view' of what is going on within a family, from a neutral, outsider position. Whilst this can be helpful taking a neutral, non-judgemental approach to some forms of destructive behaviour is seen as inadequate by critics of family therapy.

In practice, a family therapist may well suggest new ways in which family members could behave, communicate and respond to each other in order to create or introduce a more positive communication system and family environment. Ultimately, family members – and the family as a group – are responsible for making the changes that are needed for them to relate and live more harmoniously. The family therapist can promote a change in attitudes, viewpoints and behaviours within a family system but can never make this happen without co-operation and effort on the part of family members.

See also – Psychological interventions; Group therapy; Social learning theory; Therapy/therapeutic

ABC GUIDE TO PSYCHOLOGICAL PERSPECTIVES

Freud

Sigmund Freud (1856 – 1939) was an Austrian doctor who developed the theory and clinical practice of psychoanalysis. Freud first qualified as a medical practitioner, a physician, but gradually developed an interest in neurology. This led to him setting up a private medical practice for the treatment of nervous diseases in Vienna in 1886. Freud learnt a lot about human psychological development, particularly psychopathology, from the patients he treated.

Freud would sit and listen as his, mainly female, patients talked about their anxieties and fears. He learnt a lot about human psychological development, particularly psychopathology, this way. In particular, Freud's therapy sessions would often focus on the childhood memories and traumas experienced by his patients.

Early psychosexual development
Freud also believed that human beings go through several stages of psychosexual development and that early experiences play an important part in this. During this process a child's libido (energy) is focused on the part of their body relevant to that stage.

If the needs of a developing child are met at a particular stage, they can move on to the next stage. If the child struggles or experiences conflict at a particular stage of their development, they may become 'fixated'. Freud argued that this could result in their personality being shaped in a particular way.

Figure 12 – Freud's stages of psychosexual development

Stage of development	Focus	Reasons for and effects of 'fixation'
Oral (0 to 18 months)	Mouth (sucking, licking, biting)	• Child weaned too early – may develop pessimistic, sarcastic personality. • Child weaned too late - may develop gullible, naively trusting personality.
Anal (1 – 3 years)	Toilet training	• Child pressurised to begin toilet training or caught in battle of wills about it may retain faeces to deny parents control and satisfaction - may lead to obstinate, miserly or obsessive personality. • Lack of toilet training boundaries – may lead to messy, creative and disorganised personality.

ABC GUIDE TO PSYCHOLOGICAL PERSPECTIVES

Stage of development	Focus	Reasons for and effects of 'fixation'
Phallic (3 – 6 years)	Sex and gender	• Child may be filled with anxiety and guilt about unconscious rivalry with same sex parent for affection of opposite-sex parent • Boys experience 'castration anxiety', girls experience 'penis envy' • If not resolved may become homosexual / lesbian which Freud believed 'abnormal'.
Latency stage (6 – puberty)	Social pursuits e.g friendships, sport, academic achievement	• Not strictly a psychosexual development stage • Focus is on social development
Genital stage (puberty to maturity)	Sexual relationships	• More easily negotiated if no previous fixations. • If earlier conflicts resolved will have ability to form warm, loving heterosexual relationship.

See also – Psychoanalysis; Psychodynamic perspective; Defence mechanisms; Unconscious mind; Early experiences

HEALTH AND SOCIAL CARE

Genetics

Genetics is the scientific study of genes, heredity and genetic variation in living organisms.

Gregor Mendel (1822 – 1884), a 19th century priest and scientist, is seen as the originator of the modern science of genetics. The experiments he carried out on pea plants established many of the rules of heredity, which are now known as the laws of Mendelian inheritance. Mendel's big discovery was that biological traits are handed down from parents to their offspring through what he called 'units of inheritance' and which are now known as genes. He also showed that the 'dominant' or 'recessive' nature of these genes determined whether they would be expressed in the new organism.

Modern genetic science has developed beyond studying basic gene function and behaviour but does still include this as a significant focus. The structure, function and distribution of genes and their influence on various diseases, developmental processes and human behaviour is now a major part of modern genetics.

Genetic predisposition

The concept of genetic predisposition refers the capacity for human beings to inherit the potential to develop particular characteristics and diseases. Medical research has identified a number of diseases that have a genetic component – including some cancers, some forms of dementia and cardiovascular diseases. Genetic predisposition is usually due to the person inheriting one or more gene mutations or a combination of genes associated with a disease.

This puts the person at higher risk of developing (or more susceptible to) the disease than a person who has no genetic predisposition.

However, environmental and lifestyle factors (smoking, drinking to excess, being obese, lack of exercise etc) are typically required to trigger a person's genetic predisposition to a particular disease or condition. Genetic testing can now be used to identify people who are genetically predisposed to certain diseases.

Genetic transmission
Genetic transmission refers to the transmission of genes from parents to their offspring and is very closely linked to the concept of heredity. Your parents give you your unique genotype. This happens at the moment of conception when a sperm from your father fertilises an ovum, or egg, in your mother's fallopian tube. The sperm cell and the egg cell each contain their own distinctive genes, spun on a DNA ribbon, containing the instructions for life of a new human being. Conception unites these two sets of DNA, one from the father and one from the mother. This genetic material from the two parents is then mixed into a new, unique and individual combination that becomes your genetic blueprint or genotype.

Sperm cells and egg cells are made from so-called *germ cells* or gametes that are found in the male's testes and the female's ovaries. Sperm and egg cells are unlike other cells in the body in that they do *not* contain all 46 chromosomes in 23 pairs. Each germ cell has only 23 chromosomes instead of 23 *pairs* of chromosomes.

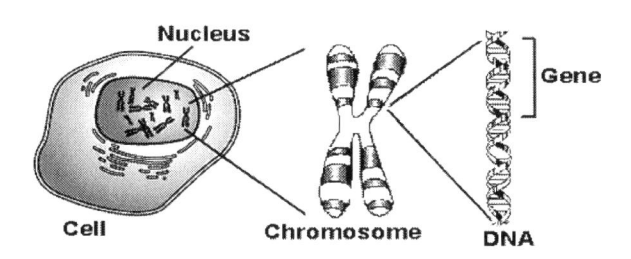

Figure 13 – Germ cells contain chromosomes which contain DNA ribbons where genes are located

When conception occurs the egg cell's 23 chromosomes and the sperm cell's 23 chromosomes combine to form the 23 pairs that will be part of each cell in the new, developing body of the foetus. Because you have pairs of chromosomes (23 from your mother and 23 from your father), you also have matching pairs of genes for nearly every biological trait. 22 of the pairs, known as autosomes, look alike and can be matched. For these 22 genes, the instructions of the dominant gene are followed rather than those of the other so-called recessive gene.

A recessive gene's instructions are only followed if neither in its pair are dominant. The features and characteristics that an individual inherits are therefore, generally those that are genetically dominant.

Suppose, for example, you inherit the gene for Type A blood from one parent and the gene for Type O blood from your other parent. In this case, the Type A gene is dominant. You will have Type A blood. Because the Type O gene is recessive, you will inherit Type O blood only if you inherit two Type O genes, one from each parent. But what about individuals who have Type AB blood? A person with Type AB blood has inherited one Type A gene from one parent and one Type B gene from the other parent. Neither of these genes dominates the other so the instructions of both come into play.

But, you're probably wondering, what about the twenty-third pair of chromosomes? These are the sex chromosomes and are different to the autosomes as they can be one of two types: X or Y chromosomes. Female egg cells only carry X chromosomes. The sperm cells from the father can carry an X *or* Y chromosome. It is therefore the father's sperm cells that determine whether the child will be male or female. If the sperm that fertilises the egg cell carries an X chromosome, the child will have an XX combination of sex chromosomes and will be female. If the sperm that fertilises the egg carries a Y chromosome, the child will have an XY combination of sex chromosomes and will be male.

HEALTH AND SOCIAL CARE

The complexity of genetic inheritance

In the example above about how blood type is inherited, we explained heredity in a relatively simple way. It may have appeared that a person's physical traits or characteristics result from the influence of single dominant genes. This isn't quite true. Many human characteristics are the result of a combination of genes. Hair colour, eye colour and temperament, for example, are all affected by lots of pairs of genes working together. Advances in genetic research are continually revealing how complex combinations work. Nevertheless, scientific understanding of the processes of genetic inheritance and the significance of biological factors in human development is far from complete.

On a biological, or physical, level it is fair to say that genes do exert a powerful influence on human growth and development. In other areas of human development – notably, psychological and social development – we need to take account of lots of other factors alongside the influence of genes. We should also be careful about the idea that genes always have the last say on the biological level.

For example, whilst we might inherit a genetic predisposition to cancer or heart disease, our lifestyle can aggravate or lessen the risk of disease occurring. So, while genes play an important role in who we are and what we become, the circumstances of our lives and the decisions we make are also very influential.

See also – Maturational theory; Nature versus Nurture; Biological psychology; Developmental norms

Group therapy

Group therapy is a type of psychotherapy that involves a therapist (or a team of therapists) working with several people (a group) who have similar problems or shared interests. In addition to the psychological interventions that occur within the group, the communication, social interactions and relationship dynamics between group members and the group leaders play an important part in the therapeutic process.

Group therapy generally involves six to ten people meeting regularly with one or two group therapists. There can be a variety of different reasons and purposes for meeting. Groups can be used to deliver different forms of psychological therapy, including cognitive-behavioural, interpersonal and psychodynamic therapies. However, the term 'group therapy' is generally associated with forms of group psychotherapy that are based on psychodynamic / psychoanalytic theories and techniques.

A general assumption of group psychotherapy is that the interactions between people in the group will replicate the problems that brought them to group therapy in the first place. As a result, the processes and dynamics of the group can be used to illustrate and understand these problems and are also a mechanism for changing the attitudes, feelings and behaviour of group members. In some cases, group therapy has a purely supportive purpose. It is used to give people who have had similar (often negative or difficult) experiences opportunities to share these experiences with others who are likely to be understanding and supportive.

Alternatively, a group may be used to find out about and try out different, more positive ways of relating to other people. For example, a person may share their feelings of low self-esteem and lack of confidence but go on to test out different ways of being assertive within the group.

The role of the group therapist is to analyse and monitor the dynamics of the group, facilitate communication and enable members to participate in a safe, supported and productive way. Groups usually negotiate rules relating to confidentiality, boundaries and ways of working that the therapist and group members must always adhere to.

Group therapy is a common feature of both statutory and voluntary mental health and social care settings and is also now often available in private counselling and psychotherapy settings. In addition to 'talking therapy' groups, group therapy may be delivered through dance, drama / psychodrama, music and art therapy groups. Specialist therapeutic community settings, where people live together as a group, also make explicit use of group therapy approaches. In these settings the total environment or milieu of the setting is use as the therapy medium. All workers and members of the therapeutic community are part of the group. Their daily activities and interactions are the focus of regular analysis and discussion, often at a weekly 'community meeting'. Group members can use these meetings to raise issues, make comments about what has been happening or criticise how they have been treated or even be confronted about their attitudes and behaviour towards others.

See also – Family therapy; Therapy/therapeutic; Cognitive Behavioural Therapy; Addiction therapy

Humanistic perspective

The humanist perspective is one of the major approaches used within contemporary academic and applied psychology to understand and explain human behaviour and psychological experience. Its key claim is that the whole person needs to be understood, not just one aspect of their psychological functioning.

The humanistic perspective became popular in psychology and began to influence health and social care practitioners from the mid-twentieth century onwards. Abraham Maslow (1908 – 1970) and Carl Rogers (1902 – 1987), both American psychologists, are now seen as the pioneers of this perspective. The humanistic perspective adopts an holistic approach to human experience. This involves studying the whole person rather than focusing on a specific aspect or part of them. It is concerned with uniquely human issues and experiences such as the self, self-actualisation (achieving your potential) and individuality.

There is now wide acceptance in the health and social care sectors that an individual's needs, identity and preferences should always be respected. It is good practice not to criticise or make personal judgements about people who are receiving care, for example. Humanistic psychologists argue that we need to try to identify with other individuals – which can be difficult because of social differences – in order to avoid discriminatory practice and to provide services that meet each individual's needs and preferences. In this way the humanistic principle of valuing the personal worth of each individual is being put into practice.

The strengths and weaknesses or limitations of the humanistic approach to psychology are summarised in the table below.

Strengths	Weaknesses / limitations
1. Recognises the complexity of human emotions and relationships affects the way people develop and behave.	1. Based on relatively vague, unscientific concepts that can't be tested easily.
2. Provides useful concepts for developing supportive and ethical human relationships.	2. Encourages people to focus on self-fulfilment and perfecting themselves – it can be seen as narcissistic.
3. Sees people as capable of resolving their problems in an individual way.	3. Focuses on the individual rather than on the influence of others or their broader social or cultural surroundings.
4. The humanistic perspective encouraged psychologists to accept that there is more to human behaviour and psychological experience than observable behaviour.	4. The humanistic focus on the individual and self-fulfilment can be seen as selfish and narcissistic.
5. Humanism is based on a positive view of human nature that emphasises individual responsibility.	5. Critics see the humanistic perspective as an overly optimistic view of the world. It doesn't recognise that some people are unable to achieve self-fulfilment because of significant social disadvantages, for example.

Strengths	Weaknesses / limitations
6. The ideas and concepts of the humanistic perspective are flexible and can be applied widely in health and social care settings.	6. The ideas and theories of the humanistic perspective can't be tested. They are seen as vague and unverifiable by those who want scientific evidence of effectiveness.
7. The humanistic perspective is based on values that are inclusive and supportive of all human beings.	7. The humanistic perspective suggests that everyone is capable of achieving self-actualisation and self-fulfilment. This may only be true of very talented and socially advantaged people.
8. The humanistic perspective is very client-centred and has enabled a large counselling industry to grow and develop.	8. Humanistic psychology ignores the unconscious – it recognises only those thoughts and behaviours that people are aware of.

See also – Active listening; Empathy; Maslow's Hierarchy of Needs; Self-actualisation; Rogers, Carl; Self-concept; Self-esteem; Self-fulfilling prophecy

References
Rogers, C. (1963) *On Becoming a Person: A therapist's view of psychotherapy*, London, Constable

HEALTH AND SOCIAL CARE

Influence

Influence is a concept that has been investigated, explored and theorised about within social psychology. From a psychological perspective, influence occurs when a person's emotions, attitudes and opinions and behaviour is affected by others.

There are a number of different types or forms of social influence. These include conformity, obedience, peer pressure and the self-fulfilling prophecy. Psychologists, educators and health and social care workers often employ the psychology of social influence to engage, maintain relationships with and ensure the effective provision and management of treatment and support for service users. An understanding of the different forms of social influence and the way they affect behaviour can help health and social care practitioners to understand how and why their clients (and co-workers) act, respond and think in different situations.

See also – Conformity; Obedience; Self-fulfilling prophecy

Learning difficulties

Learning difficulties is a term used within educational and child care settings to refer to one or more problems that an individual has with acquiring knowledge and skills to the level expected of people of their age.

Learning *disability* rather than learning difficulty is now used to indicate that a person has an intellectual impairment that affects their overall ability to function (socially and psychologically) and learn. The contemporary focus on learning *disability* shifts attention away from a person's IQ or level of intelligence to their general social functioning, ability to acquire new skills and understand information and their ability to live independently.

The term learning difficulty is used to focus attention directly and specifically on a problem related to learning rather than on social or psychological functioning. A person may have a generalised learning difficulty that may or may not be linked to their level of intelligence. For example, a child who has a visual or hearing impairment or a physical disability that restricts their ability to access standard educational facilities and resources may experience learning difficulties in mainstream educational settings and may be identified as having special educational needs. Alternatively, a person may have a specific learning difficulty, such as dyslexia, that has no link to their IQ but which affects their ability to learn.

See also – Cognitive perspective; Challenging behaviour; Developmental norms

HEALTH AND SOCIAL CARE

Maslow's hierarchy of needs

Abraham Maslow (1908 – 1970) was an American psychologist who used a humanistic approach in his work on human needs and motivation. He is most well-known for his theory of psychological health and development that is based on the innate human drive to fulfil a hierarchy of needs.

As a psychologist, Abraham Maslow (1943) was particularly interested in motivation and the way this affects human behaviour. He wanted to show that humans are not blindly reacting to situations or stimuli as behaviourism implies. He believed that a person's behaviour and development is needs-driven. You are probably already aware of Maslow's idea that human behaviour is linked to a 'hierarchy of needs'.

Self-actualisation
(Achieving individual potential)

Esteem
(self-esteem and esteem from others)

Belonging
(Love, affection, being a part of groups)

Safety
(Shelter, removal from danger)

Physiological
(Health, food, sleep)

Figure 14 - Maslow's Hierarchy of Needs

Maslow's humanistic approach to development and behaviour is based on the belief that human beings have a number of different types of 'need' and that these needs must be met or satisfied in a particular sequence before the person can develop further. Specifically, a person's basic physiological needs must be met first before they can satisfy their safety and security needs. Their behaviour will then be motivated by a desire to satisfy their love and emotional needs. When these are satisfied, the person will be motivated to meet their self-esteem needs. At this point, the individual is in a position to focus on achieving their full potential or need for self-actualisation.

Maslow's contribution to the humanistic perspective focuses on the way in which human behaviour and development is motivated by distinctly human qualities and needs. His concept of a hierarchy of needs has been a major influence on health and social care workers since the mid-twentieth century. The belief that an individual's basic physiological and safety needs must be prioritized in the way that care is provided remains central to medical and nursing practice. Similarly, health and social care workers supporting people with non-physical social and emotional problems often draw on Maslow's insights to create support and treatment plans based on the idea that people are motivated to behave, develop and change in a needs-based way.

See also – Humanistic perspective; Self-actualisation; Nature versus Nurture

References
Maslow, A. (1943) *Motivation and Personality*, New York, Harper and Row

Maturational Theory

Maturational theory is a biologically-based approach to human development. It is most closely associated with Arnold Gessell (1880 – 1961), an American psychologist and paediatrican.

Gessell outlined a theory of human development based on the claim that human development occurs in response to a sequence of biologically-based changes in the human body – especially the brain. The individual is seen as maturing through several different but linked stages of growth and development in which a predictable, biologically-based 'programme' of maturation unfolds. For example, foetal development during pregnancy follows a fixed, predictable set of stages until the foetus is ready to be born. From birth, a genetic 'programme' leads to the baby developing into a child and the child into an adolescent. Maturational processes then lead on to developmental changes occurring in adulthood and finally a progression into old age.

Gessell claimed that this process of change and development follows a relatively predictable pattern because it is 'hard wired' into the human genome. From this perspective, maturational processes drive human physical, psychological and emotional development with the environment providing only background support rather than playing a leading role. This contrasts with the humanistic and social learning perspectives where nurture effects are seen as having a paramount influence on the individual's development.

See also – Genetics; Biological psychology; Nervous system; Endocrine system

Mental illness

'Mental illness' is a biomedical / psychiatric concept that defines experiences of significant emotional distress, disordered thinking and extreme or bizarre behaviours as abnormal and the result of biologically-based illness or disease.

The concept of mental illness is controversial and disputed. Some health and social care practitioners do see mental health problems as a form of illness. Others, using psychological and social perspectives, argue that an 'illness approach' is inaccurate and unhelpful in understanding the emotional and psychological difficulties or problems that people diagnosed with forms of 'mental illness' experience.

The following list of terms can all be used to indicate that a person is experiencing some sort of 'mental' disorder or difficulty in relation to their feelings, behaviour and / or mental experiences:
- Mental health problems
- Mental illness
- Mental distress
- Mental disorder
- Madness
- Psychological problems
- Psychiatric problems

All of these terms are likely to be familiar to health and social care workers practising in mental health settings. They would also recognise that 'mental illness' and 'psychiatric problems' are the terms that psychiatrists and other medical practitioners are most likely to use.

Psychiatry and the causes of mental illness

Psychiatry is a branch of medicine dealing with disorders in which mental or behavioural features are most prominent (Davies 1997). Psychiatry provides a set of beliefs and concepts about emotional and psychological difficulties based on medical ideas of 'illness' and 'disorder'. These ideas, and the mental health-care practices that result from them, are dominant within the statutory and private sector mental health systems in the UK and in developed, Westernised countries generally.

Medically qualified psychiatrists tend to believe that mental illnesses originate from biological dysfunction. These include dysfunction of the brain, malfunctioning biochemical processes and the inheritance of 'faulty' genes that predispose people to mental illnesses. Psychiatrists who base their health-care practice on biological psychiatry identify mental illness as being located within the individual who experiences mental 'distress' and exhibits symptoms of behavioural and/or emotional 'disorder'. As a result, biologically orientated forms of psychiatry tend to underplay, and in more extreme cases ignore, the possible contribution and impact of other non-biological factors (cultural, social, psychological and spiritual, for example) in the causation of mental health problems.

Diagnosis of 'mental illness'

The psychiatric diagnosis of mental illness is similar to the diagnosis of physical health problems. Practitioners of both psychiatric and physical medicine tend to look for evidence of 'abnormality' within an individual. However, where practitioners of physical medicine carry out examinations, tests, X-rays and other scans to identify objective signs of physical 'abnormality' (high blood pressure, unusual pulse rates, 'abnormal' biochemistry results, tumours, fractures, bruising and bleeding, for example), psychiatrists can't directly see mental 'abnormality'. The 'mind', unlike the physical anatomy of the body, can't be located or directly observed. As a result, psychiatric practitioners look for patterns of behaviour and subjective 'symptoms' (low mood, poor sleep, loss of appetite, lack of energy, unusual or distressing thoughts) to diagnose 'mental illness'.

Figure 15 – Examples of medical categories of mental illness

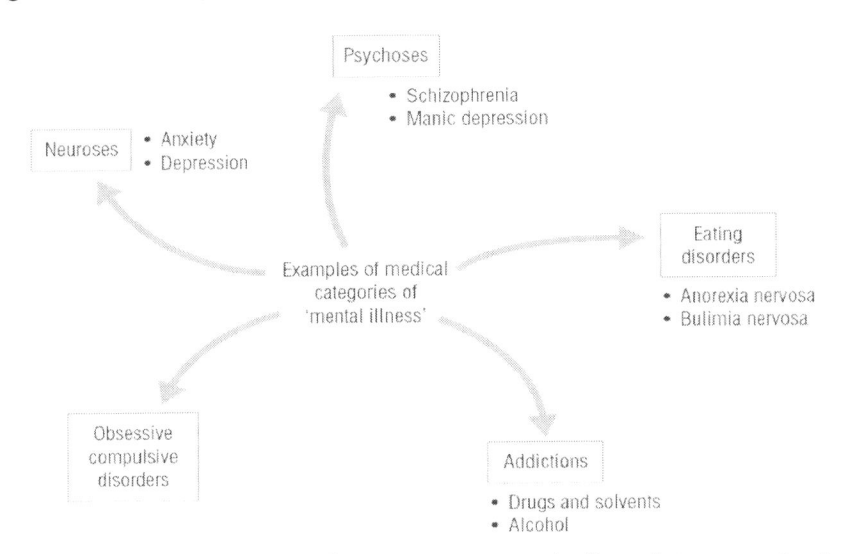

Examples of medical categories of 'mental illness':

- Psychoses
  - Schizophrenia
  - Manic depression
- Neuroses
  - Anxiety
  - Depression
- Eating disorders
  - Anorexia nervosa
  - Bulimia nervosa
- Obsessive compulsive disorders
- Addictions
  - Drugs and solvents
  - Alcohol

Particular combinations of symptoms are believed to equate to different 'mental illnesses'. A number of mental illness classification systems exist. The International Classification of Diseases (ICD) system is probably the best known and is widely used by psychiatrists in the UK.

The power of the psychiatric perspective is such that its illness framework is often taken-for-granted as a valid and helpful way of understanding mental distress. It is widely used by general and mental health professionals as well as by members of the public as a language for thinking and talking about experiences of mental distress in contemporary society. As a result, the influence of general practitioners, psychiatrists and other care practitioners is powerful in determining what is and what is not considered to be a mental health problem. These people can define experiences and behaviour as evidence of illness, and their expertise and authority are likely to be called on to confirm the opinion of lay people that their relative, friend or colleague has 'gone mad' (Rogers and Pilgrim, 2010).

Criticism of psychiatry

Critics of psychiatry challenge the medical claim that people experiencing mental distress have a mental 'illness' and that this is likely to be caused by factors within the individual (such as a 'broken brain'). There are many different critics of psychiatry who dispute the 'illness' approach to mental distress. These include the service user movement, mental health practitioners who use non-medical ways of understanding and explaining mental distress and academics who question the validity of 'mental illness' as a concept and claim it is a 'myth'.

Is 'mental illness' a myth?

Thomas Szasz (1961) first contested the claim that physical and mental illness are similar phenomena. Despite being a psychiatrist himself, Szasz argued that the term 'mental illness' is an inappropriate description of the mental distress that people experience. Instead, Szasz viewed 'mental illness' as a socially constructed myth maintained by the psychiatric profession. This is a controversial claim, given the widespread use and acceptance of psychiatric definitions of 'mental illness'. Szasz (1971) argued that mental distress is not the result of 'disease' or objective abnormality in the way that physical illness is. He argued that people who are diagnosed as suffering from 'mental illness' are really experiencing 'problems in living'. These are essentially social problems, not biomedical problems. Szasz saw 'mental illness' as a metaphor, not a 'fact'. He saw it as a way of dealing with people whose behaviour, beliefs and thoughts 'violate certain ethical, political and social norms' (Szasz 1974, p. 23). As a result, Szasz (1974) saw the institutional, organised forms of psychiatric care as being repressive, coercive and performing a social control function in modern society.

It is important to note that Szasz (1974) and other critics of psychiatry are not denying the existence of mental distress or saying that psychological and emotional problems are not important. They are saying that these experiences aren't 'illnesses' in the way medical practitioners claim they are.

See also – Anxiety; Depression; Eating disorders; Phobias; Post Traumatic Stress Disorder;

References
Rogers, A. and Pilgrim, D. (2010), *A Sociology of Mental Health and Illness*, Palgrave Macmillan
Szasz, T. (1961) *The Myth of Mental Illness,* Routledge & Kegan Paul, London
Szasz, T, (1971), *The Manufacture of Madness*, Routledge & Kegan Paul, London
Szasz, T. (1974), *Ideology and Insanity*, Penguin, Harmondsworth

HEALTH AND SOCIAL CARE

Nature versus Nurture debate

The nature-nurture debate contrasts two important ways of explaining human growth and development:

- the 'nature' approach suggests that people are born with qualities, abilities and characteristics that determine the kind of person they will become.

- the 'nurture' approach argues that it is the way a person is brought up and the circumstances they live in that are a more important influence on the kind of person they become.

Nature influences on human growth and development include genetic factors and biological processes that affect the person from within. People who take a more extreme 'nature' viewpoint, argue that we are pre-programmed by our genes and biological processes to develop and behave in certain ways. By contrast, nurture influences are non-biological, environmental factors that affect the person from outside. People who take a more extreme 'nurture' viewpoint argue that human beings are not programmed to develop in a specific way because we have free will, can make lifestyle choices and are influenced by a complex range of psychological, social, geographic and economic factors.

The nature-nurture debate is often presented as an argument between two extreme viewpoints. However, psychologists and health and social care practitioners are now more likely to adopt a third approach that takes account of both types of influence:

- Biological influences (nature) are important for *universal* forms of development (e.g learning to walk)

- Environmental influences (nurture) are prominent in particular forms of development (e.g learning to speak with a particular local accent).

If you agree with this third approach, you would accept that genes enable most of us to walk but only a person brought up in a particular area is likely to develop a genuine local accent.

Evaluating the impact of nature and nurture influences

Nature and nurture influences on human growth and development can be thought of as 'internal' and 'external' influences. Internal (nature) factors, such as genes, determine how a person grows and develops because they have a direct, biological influence on the person. These internal nature-type influences tend to have their strongest impact on growth and development during infancy, adolescence and old age. Basic, biological processes cause irreversible physical changes to the human body during these life stages.

External environmental (nurture) influences, on the other hand, have a less direct effect on human growth and development. They tend to shape rather than determine a person's emotional, social and intellectual development and life course. External environmental influences are important, for example, in promoting social development during childhood and adolescence, and emotional development during infancy and adolescence.

See also – Genetics; Maturational theory; Endocrine system; Nervous system; Culture

Nervous system

The human nervous system is a network of nerve cells and fibres that transmit nerve impulses (signals or 'messages') between different parts of the body.

The nervous system consists of:

- The brain and spinal cord (the central nervous system or CNS)
- The nerves running through the body (the peripheral nervous system)
- The autonomic nervous system (this controls the heart rate, contraction of smooth muscle in the gut and some endocrine glands)
- The sense organs (for example the eyes and ears)
- Internal sense organs (chemoreceptors that can detect chemicals like carbon dioxide in the blood)

What is the nervous system made of?
The central nervous system or CNS includes the brain and spinal cord. It contains two main types of tissues:
- Grey matter which is made up of the cell bodies of nerve cell
- White matter which includes all the fibres running between nerve cells and other organs

The grey matter in the brain covers the outer surface and has the job of 'thinking' – it is our grey matter that makes us 'smart'. Different parts of the brain do different jobs but they all depend on good connections.

These connections are the nerve fibres. They carry nerve impulses across the nervous system. Each fibre is insulated from the ones next to it by a thin covering of myelin. It is the myelin which makes the white matter look white. The peripheral nervous system includes the nerves that run out of the spine. These nerves are paired so that nerves leaving on the right hand side of the spine match nerves leaving on the left.

Biological psychology and behaviour
Biological psychologists have a strong interest in the nervous system. In particular, they often study the ways that different part of the brain, such as the right and left hemispheres, operate and affect human functioning. Movement, language and emotion are all influenced by particular parts of the brain, for example. When an area of the brain is damaged, or temporarily impaired by illness, drugs or other substances, a person's behaviour and mental abilities can be affected. Characteristic behaviour (tremors, impulsiveness or disinhibition, for example) can occur or the person can lose some functional ability (speech, memory, judgement).

Neurotransmitter	**Psychological effects**
Low serotonin levels	Increased risk of depression, suicide, impulsive aggression and alcoholism
High serotonin levels	Link to fearfulness, obsessive behaviour, shyness and lack of self-confidence
High dopamine levels	Increased risk of schizophrenia and experience of hallucinations

HEALTH AND SOCIAL CARE

Biological psychologists are also very interested in physiological processes, particularly the influence of neurotransmitters, on behaviour and mental state. Serotonin and dopamine are two neurotransmitters that are thought to have a strong influence on a person's mental state (see table below).

See also – Biological psychology; Depression; Biofeedback

Obedience

In psychological terms, obedience is a form of conformity to authority.

The psychological experiments of Stanley Milgram (1963) and Phillip Zimbardo (1973) established that obedience to authority is a basic, deeply ingrained psychological response, even when actions based on obedience can lead to others apparently being mistreated or even harmed. This finding has led to a lot of subsequent psychological research and is an important issue for health and social care workers employed to support and safeguard vulnerable people. In particular, care practitioners need to be aware of the impact that an imbalance in power in care relationships and the deference some clients pay to the status and 'expertise' of health and social care workers can have. Health and social care workers who use professional authority to make clients obey them, are unlikely to be working in a respectful, constructive partnership that recognises the individual's rights and particular needs. Instead, they are likely to create a situation that is disempowering, controlling and belittling of the individual.

See also – Social learning theory; Role theory; Role models

References
Milgram, S. (1963). Behavioral study of obedience. *Journal of Abnormal and Social Psychology* **67**: 371–378.
Haney, C; Banks, C.; Zimbardo, P. (1973). Interpersonal dynamics in a simulated prison. *International Journal of Criminology and Penology* **1**: 69–97.

HEALTH AND SOCIAL CARE

Operant conditioning

Operant conditioning is a form of behavioural learning that occurs when the likelihood of spontaneously occurring behaviour is either increased or diminished through the use of positive or negative reinforcement.

This aspect of behaviourism is associated with B.F. Skinner who used experiments with rats and pigeons to develop his instrumental learning theory. Skinner built a special box – now known as 'Skinner box' – to facilitate the learning of new behaviours. The box contained a lever which when pressed released a food pellet or 'reward' to the rat in the box. After some trial and error, the rat learned that lever pressing had a consequence – it would be rewarded with food.

Skinner believed that the reward reinforced the rat's lever-pressing behaviour and made it more likely that this behaviour would be repeated, or occur again, in the future. It is because the rat requires a 'reward' to repeat their behaviour that this is also called instrumental learning.

Understanding operant conditioning

Skinner's theory of operant conditioning is based on the idea that learning takes place through reinforcement. Skinner identified two types of reinforcement:

- positive reinforcement where the consequences following a behaviour are experienced as desirable
- negative reinforcement where carrying out a behaviour removes something unpleasant.

It is important to know that negative reinforcement and punishment are not the same things. Punishment occurs when behaviour is followed by consequences that are unpleasant. For example, slapping a child who misbehaves is physical punishment for being 'naughty'. However, behaving well in order to avoid being sent to bed early is negative reinforcement. Negative reinforcement is used to make something happen whereas punishment is used to stop something happening.

See also – Behaviourism; Classical conditioning; Conditioning; Reinforcement; Pavlov, Ivan

HEALTH AND SOCIAL CARE

Pavlov, Ivan

Ivan Pavlov (1849 – 1936) was a Russian physiologist who discovered and developed the laws of classical conditioning.

During experiments that were originally designed to investigate the process of digestion in dogs, Pavlov accidentally discovered that animal behaviours develop partly through 'associative learning'. Pavlov's discovery changed the belief that animal behaviours were largely instinctive. The relatively simple approach to promoting learning that Pavlov developed is now known as 'classical conditioning'.

See also – Behaviourism; Conditioning; Classical conditioning; Reinforcement

Personal constructs

Personal constructs are ways of seeing the world that are unique to each individual. An individual is said to create their personal constructs out of their experience of the world and uses them to interpret, predict and make sense of what is, or might be, happening around them.

George Kelly (1905 – 1966), an American psychologist, first used a cognitive approach to develop Personal Construct Theory. He saw the individual as a 'scientist' making predictions about the future, testing them and revising or acting on them according to 'evidence'. Personal construct theory claims that people have to develop constructs to interpret and make sense of the environment in which they live. Because our environments are continually changing, we have to process lots of information and integrate it into the way we think about the world. We do this by developing and using new constructs in an adaptive way. Kelly argued that people (re)construct a future for themselves, and even 'reinvent' themselves, by changing their habitual ways of thinking about themselves and their environment.

See also – Cognitive behavioural therapy; Cognitive perspective

Person-centred counselling

Person-centred counselling is an approach to psychological intervention and support that draws on and puts into practice a range of concepts and techniques developed by humanistic psychologists and practitioners.

The goal of person-centred counselling is to support and enable the individual to develop a sense of self that gives them insight into how their attitudes, emotions and behaviours affect the way they relate to others and experience the world more generally. Carl Roger's person-centred approach to counselling is now widely used and very influential in the health and social care sector. Rogers (1961) identified the three conditions of genuineness, empathy and unconditional positive regard as fundamental to effective therapeutic communication.

- Genuineness involves being yourself and contributing to interactions and relationships with honesty and integrity. Health and social care workers who are genuine in their interactions avoid being authoritarian, defensive or professionally detached.
- Empathy involves the ability to see and experience situations from another person's perspective.
- Unconditional positive regard involves accepting and validating an individual's experiences, feelings, beliefs and judgements unconditionally and in a non-judgemental way.

ABC GUIDE TO PSYCHOLOGICAL PERSPECTIVES

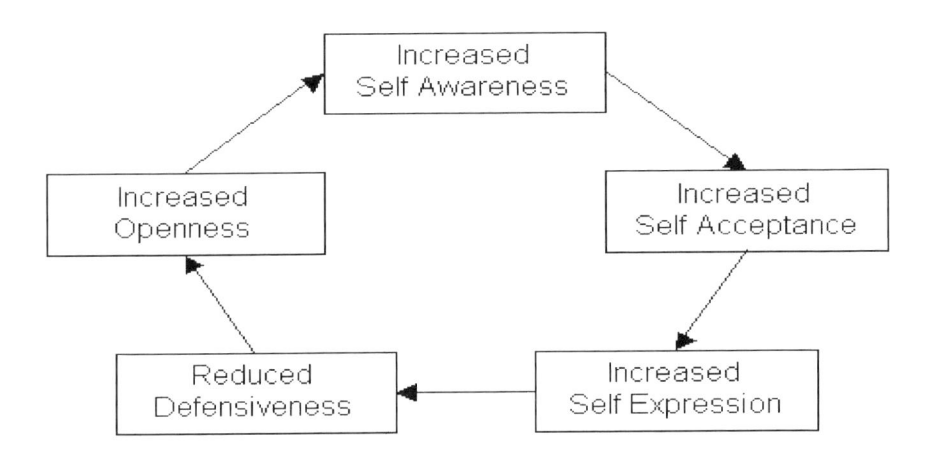

```
        Increased Self Awareness
       ↗                    ↘
Increased              Increased
Openness              Self Acceptance
   ↑                        ↓
Reduced        ←      Increased
Defensiveness         Self Expression
```

Figure 16 – The goals of person-centred counselling

Non-judgemental acceptance of people enables health and social care workers to connect with the real, unique people they care for and support. Similarly, those who use a person-centred approach to counselling use genuineness, empathy and unconditional positive regard to help the person they are working with develop a positive self-image and greater self-acceptance.

See also – Humanistic perspective; Active listening; Empathy; Self-concept; Self-esteem

References
Rogers, C. (1961) *On Becoming a Person: A Therapists view of psychotherapy*, London, Constable.

HEALTH AND SOCIAL CARE

Phobias

In a very basic way, a phobia is an intense, irrational fear of something that poses little or no danger.

As a psychological term phobia is used to define and describe a particular form of anxiety-based problem. 'Phobia' is also sometimes used in everyday, popular language to convey a dislike about or desire to avoid a situation, object or person ('He's got a computer phobia') but this is an inaccurate and misleading use of it. A person may be diagnosed with a phobia by a medical or mental health practitioner or by a clinical psychologist if their irrational fear and avoidant behaviour is dysfunctional. A diagnosis may be given if the person's fear (of open spaces, confined spaces or social situations, for example) is unfounded, causes them severe and persistent distress and has a negative, detrimental effect on their everyday behaviour and functioning. Obtaining a diagnosis is necessary before a referral for treatment can be made to psychiatric or psychological services.

Phobias are anxiety-based disorders that can be effectively treated with cognitive behavioural therapy or behaviour modification techniques such as systematic desensitisation. This involves reducing and ultimately removing the power of a maladaptive association by gradually exposing the person to the thing they are frightened of. To do this the care practitioner and the phobic person first create a 'hierarchy of fear'. The treatment stage involves gradually exposing the person to varying degrees of fear whilst also helping them to relax and cope with each exposure.
The goal is for the person to face the situation or object that they are fearful of or phobic about without worrying.

Systematic desensitisation has been used effectively to help people overcome all kinds of phobias, from agoraphobia (fear of open spaces) to arachnophobia (fear of spider), that cause distress and disrupt people's lives

See also – Anxiety, PTSD; Mental illness; Therapy / therapeutic; Behaviourism; Classical conditioning

Piaget, Jean

Jean Piaget (1896 -1980) was a Swiss psychologist who pioneered the cognitive approach in his work on children's thinking and learning. Piaget believed that children's thinking and intelligence developed over time as a result of biological maturation. He developed a stage-based theory of cognitive development in which each stage of intellectual development built on a previous one.

Figure 17 – Piaget's stages of cognitive development.

Stage	Age	Focus of development
Stage 1 Sensorimotor	0 – 2	The world is experienced via motor activity and the senses
Stage 2 Preoperational	2 – 7	Language develops with memory, the child is egocentric and unable to conserve
Stage 3 Concrete operational	7 – 11	The child can understand conservation (the ability to think logically) but can't solve problems mentally
Stage 4 Formal operational	11+	The child can use abstract thoughts and represent problems.

Piaget's theory claims that cognitive development occurs when the child's brain has matured so that it is 'ready' for development. He argued that new information and experiences are gradually assimilated into the child's existing thinking. When this happens, new experiences are accommodated by modifying existing thinking.

See also – Cognitive perspective; Nature versus Nurture

Post-traumatic stress disorder (PTSD)

Post-traumatic stress disorder (PTSD) is a mental health problem experienced by people who have been exposed to traumatic and frightening events. Typically, this includes soldiers, victims of crime and people who have suffered serious abuse.

An individual suffering PTSD will become emotionally distressed and often very frightened when a stimulus that reminds them of the traumatic event (a car backfiring = gun fire, an unexplained noise downstairs = burglar) causes them to re-experience it. As a result, people with PTSD are often very anxious, have poor sleep and poor concentration and may be hyper-vigilant (extremely watchful and alert to danger) because they believe the event could recur. This may lead to them using avoidance strategies, becoming withdrawn and estranged from others, and developing maladaptive feelings and behaviours, as ways of coping.

Mental health workers who support and treat people suffering from PTSD, try to get them to make new associations (about the event and its consequences), reframing their thoughts in a way that leaves the traumatic event in the past. The goal is to ensure that the person doesn't feel the events are recurring. Classical and operant conditioning techniques are combined in this kind of behavioural treatment. They remove the association between fear-inducing stimuli and the past event whilst also minimising and controlling the physiological effects of fear, panic and anxiety through systematic desensitisation.

See also – Anxiety; Cognitive perspective

HEALTH AND SOCIAL CARE

Prejudice and discrimination

A prejudice is an opinion, feeling or attitude, often of dislike concerning another individual or group of people.

Prejudices are typically based on inaccurate information or unreasonable judgements. They are often learnt in childhood or through secondary socialisation in peer groups, school or the workplace. When a person acts on a prejudice, they become involved in discrimination.

Prejudice is revealed and expressed through the things people say and the way they behave towards individuals or groups who are different in some way. For example, prejudice:

- Is often expressed through derogatory name-calling and by drawing attention to any physical differences, such as skin colour, facial and bodily features and behaviours.
- Thrives where there is uncertainty, anxiety and fear about an individual, or group who are different, or unfamiliar in some way.
- Asserts that people are less intelligent, less able or abnormal because of their differences.
- Claims a person is inferior - less valuable, less worthy of attention and less deserving - because of their differences.
- States that a person is wrong and unnatural, rather than just different.

The expression of prejudice can range from petty insults to extreme violence towards individuals, or groups who are different in some way. It can be expressed through unfair or unkind treatment, or by isolating and excluding a person or group. You have a responsibility to recognise discrimination and prejudice at work and to encourage understanding, by providing an inclusive setting where each person is valued.

See also – Humanistic perspective; Social learning theory; Cognitive processes; Role models

Psychoanalysis

Psychoanalysis is a system of psychological theory and clinical practices that focuses on analysis of the relationships and dynamics of an individual's conscious and unconscious mental processes. Psychoanalysis is an intensive individual therapy that is often carried out for a considerable period of time.

Psychoanalysis is mostly closely associated with Sigmund Freud (1856- 1939), though it has been developed and practised since the late nineteenth century by a number of other theorists and practitioners (Jung, Adler, etc). Psychoanalysis is both a set of theories about the structure and functioning of the human mind and an approach to psychological therapy. Psychoanalytical psychologists focus on the emotional and personality aspects of human development rather than on the learning or intellectual areas that cognitive theorists explore.

Psychoanalysis and personality

The word 'personality' comes from the Latin word 'persona'. This describes the mask worn during theatrical dramas. It refers to the relatively stable and enduring aspects of the individual that distinguish him or her from other people. Effectively, every human being develops a unique personality and identity. The development of personality is a dynamic and evolving process. Things are always changing and developing even though the qualities of an individual's personality remains relatively consistent over time.

Freud was interested in, and proposed a theory to explain, how human personality is structured and how it develops. Freud believed that the mind consisted of three 'territories'. These are the conscious; the pre-conscious; and the unconscious parts of the mind. The conscious mind is aware of the here and now, functioning when the individual is awake to behave in a rational, thoughtful way. The pre-conscious mind contains partially forgotten ideas and feelings. It also prevents unacceptable, disturbing unconscious memories from surfacing. The unconscious mind is the biggest part and acts as a store of all the memories, feelings and ideas that the individual experiences throughout their life.

The things that lurk deep in the unconscious are seen to play a powerful, ongoing role in influencing the individual's emotions, behaviour and personality.

Freud also believed that the development and expression of an individual's emotions and behaviour is driven by the operation of what he called the Id, Ego and Super-Ego. The Id is a raw mass of powerful, unruly energies that are pleasure-seeking and demand 'satisfaction'. The operation of the Id is unconscious but is continually seeking outlets. The Id is most powerful and is least checked when we are in our infancy. Newborn babies are completely dependent on others to satisfy their needs. The powerful, demanding Id causes the baby to kick and scream and react angrily when it's needs aren't met immediately. The simple pleasure-seeking of the Id has to be controlled if the individual is to adjust to a society in which they are not the 'centre of the universe' and will have to compromise, share and accept that they can't always have what they want when they want it.

The development of the individual's Ego begins when the child becomes aware that she will have to adjust her demands to fit in with the world around her. The Super Ego develops later when the child incorporates the standards of behaviour of people whose approval she values. The Super-Ego is like the child's conscience as it acts like an internal control on impulsive behaviour.

Psychoanalysis and psychosexual development

Freud's theories suggest that human development evolves as an individual progresses through stages in which the basic instinctual sexual energy (called the libido) seeks expression in ways that are progressively more sophisticated. When Freud used the term 'sexual energy' he meant it in the broad sense of any pleasurable bodily sensation. This obviously includes the current, everyday use of the phrase but also refers to acts such as eating.

According to Freud, the greatest source of pleasure for a young infant is being fed. During feeding, particularly breast-feeding, the child's attention becomes focused on the person providing the nourishment. In most cases, this is the mother. Freud referred to early infancy (from birth to age one) as the oral stage of a child's development.

This is when the baby's oral organs – lips, mouth and tongue – are its main means for obtaining the sensory (and 'sexual') pleasure of feeding. Freudian theory claims that a happy, balanced oral stage can tilt a child towards a happy adulthood. On the other hand, insufficient or excessive gratification during the oral stage, can lead to psychological problems in later life. For example, over-indulgence can 'spoil' a child, resulting in an over-dependent adult.

During the second year of life, the anus and defecation become important sources of sensory (and 'sexual') pleasure for the child. Interactions between child and parents concerning toilet training take on special significance. It's at this time, from the age of one to three – the anal stage – that other adult predispositions are formed. For example, refusing to defecate when it's appropriate to do so, can lead to obsessive cleanliness in adulthood. Toilet training routines cause the child to experience restrictions of the Id impulses but she also learns that she can challenge parental authority by rebelling against the training routine.

At around the age of three, the child enters the phallic stage, which lasts until age five. In this period, the child's genital organs provide the main source of sensory pleasure. During the phallic stage, children also develop a sexual desire towards the opposite sex parent, and hostility towards the same sex parent, who is seen as a sexual rival. Boys fall in love with their mother and resent their father, and girls long for their father and are jealous of their mother. This sexual attachment to opposite sex parents and hostility towards same sex parents is known, in the case of the boy, as the Oedipus complex, and, in the case of the girl, as the Electra complex. Faced with these powerful sexual urges, the child's mind does battle with its body's instincts.

During the struggle, the id (the impulsive instinct-driven part of the mind), is refereed by the ego (the growing self-awareness of the mind). Out of the tug-of-war, the child, fearful yet loving of the opposite sex parent, develops a superego (the conscience of the mind).

The phallic stage is followed by the latency stage, lasting from around age six to puberty. During this time, child sexuality seems to lie dormant, and children concentrate on same-sex friendships. The genital stage comes next, beginning at puberty and lasting, more or less, for the rest of a person's life. Sexual interest is reawakened, and, for most people, the pursuit of opposite sex partners is the norm. Freud viewed adolescence as the final stage of personality development that lasts for the rest of our lives but he also believed that 'the child within' never completely dies as some of the drives from our oral, anal and phallic stages remain repressed in the unconscious, occasionally being expressed.

Freud believed that individuals who had difficulty in passing through any particular stage of psychosexual development will find this reflected in their adult behaviour and personality. Unresolved oedipal conflicts may produce a person who has difficulty with authority figures and a poor sense of sexual identity. Anal personality types may show stubbornness, independence and possessiveness.

See also – Psychodynamic perspective; Freud, Sigmund; Defence mechanisms

Psychodynamic perspective

The psychodynamic perspective focuses on the deep, inner psychological aspects of human development and relationships. It is strongly associated with the work of Sigmund Freud (1856 - 1939) and the treatment of 'abnormal' behaviour.

This psychological perspective was originally developed by Freud (1920) as psychoanalysis. Freud used his experiences as a therapist with mentally disordered people to develop key psychoanalytic ideas. Freud was particularly interested in the connections between abnormal behaviour and unconscious, underlying psychological processes. The psychodynamic perspective in psychology now covers more than Freud's original psychoanalytic ideas. Other theorists and practitioners developed and extended Freud's work throughout the twentieth century. Erik Erikson (1902 – 1994) was one of these people. Inspired by Freud's work, Erikson produced a theory of psychosocial development that has influenced the work of many psychologists, educators and health and social care practitioners.

The psychodynamic perspective suggests that unconscious forces and conflicts cause psychological disturbance. They are driven by memories, feelings and past experiences that are locked away in the unconscious but 'leak out' in dreams, slips of the tongue ('Freudian slips') and displacement behaviour. Early childhood experiences are seen as particularly important in creating unresolved psychological conflicts that become locked into the unconscious.

Ego defence mechanisms

Freud believed that the ego used 'defence mechanisms' to protect itself and balance the demands of the Id and superego. Within the psychodynamic perspective, ego defence mechanisms are seen as a way of protecting the ego from distress and are used to cope with everyday life. Defence mechanisms allow us to unconsciously block out experiences that overwhelm us.

Figure 18 - Examples of ego defence mechanisms

Defence mechanism	Effect	Example
Repression	Person forgets an event or experience	No recollection of a serious car crash
Regression	Revert to an earlier stage of development	Bedwetting when sibling is born or school begins
Denial	Pushing events or emotion out of consciousness	Refusal to accept you have a substance misuse problem
Projection	Personal faults or negative feelings are attributed to someone else.	Accusing a colleague of being thoughtless when you are really feeling this way
Displacement	Redirecting desire or other strong emotions onto another person.	Shouting at your partner instead of your best friend

Ego defence mechanisms are seen as natural and normal but can cause psychological problems if they are over used too often.

Evaluating the psychodynamic approach

What does it offer?	What are its limitations?
1. Psychodynamic therapies are effective with certain types of people (articulate, introspective) and certain types of disorders (anxiety-based, linked to attachments and early experiences).	1. Psychodynamic therapies tend to focus on past experiences rather than the current difficulties a person faces.
2. Psychodynamic therapies seek out the root causes of people's problems and try to resolve them.	2. Digging deeply into a person's problems and past experiences can produce more distress (making the person feel worse) before a solution is found and symptoms are relieved.
3. The psychodynamic approach can be used with individuals or groups.	3. Psychodynamic treatment is costly and time-consuming and requires a specially trained therapist.

See also – Freud; Unconscious mind; Early experiences; Anxiety; Challenging behaviour

References – S. Freud (1920 *A General Introduction to Psychoanalysis*, London, Constable.

HEALTH AND SOCIAL CARE

Psychological interventions

A psychological intervention is an action or strategy that is used to support or bring about change in a person's psychological functioning, behaviour or mental state.

Psychological interventions are most closely associated with mental health practice but may also be a part of the work and activities of other health, social care and education practitioners. Psychological interventions generally have the aim of relieving a person's psychological or emotional symptoms, changing their behaviour or of uncovering and treating the cause of their distress or problems. However, psychological interventions that promote positive wellbeing, self-esteem, emotional development and happiness can also be developed and implemented by psychologists and other care, welfare and education practitioners.

The specific nature or form that a psychological intervention takes will depend on the psychological perspective that informs it. For example, a nurse trained in the use of cognitive behavioural therapy who is working with a depressed teenager will use different psychological interventions to a social worker supporting the parents of a child excluded from school because of behavioural problems. Psychological interventions need to be tailored to the specific needs of the individual and are most effective when there is clear consent from and collaboration with the person who experiences them.

See also – Behaviour modification; Cognitive Behavioural Therapy; Person-centred counselling; Psychoanalysis

Psychological perspective

A psychological perspective is a distinctive approach or school of thought within the broader academic discipline of Psychology. Each perspective offers a particular way of looking at psychological issues or experiences based on the concepts, theories and research evidence they generate.

The main psychological perspectives within contemporary Psychology are the:

- Behavioural perspective
- Social learning perspective
- Psychodynamic perspective
- Cognitive perspective
- Humanistic perspective
- Biological perspective.

Each of the main psychological perspectives has played an important role in the development of academic and applied psychology. They can be thought of as 'tools' in a toolbox that can be used to tackle different psychological challenges, though none of the perspectives is always best for every situation. Each approach has strengths and weaknesses and tends to be used to understand particular issues in human psychology.

See also – Behaviourism; Biological perspective; Social Learning Theory; Psychodynamic approach; Cognitive perspective; Humanistic perspective.

HEALTH AND SOCIAL CARE

Reinforcement

Reinforcement is a behavioural psychology concept that refers to any consequence that makes it more likely a person (or other non-human organism) will respond to a specific stimulus in a particular way in future.

For example, if a rat is given food for pressing a lever, it is more likely press the lever again. In this case, food is used to positively reinforce the desired lever pressing behaviour. Similarly, if a child is praised for desired behaviour, they are more likely to repeat that behaviour in future in order to receive praise again. In both of these examples, behaviour is being positively reinforced through rewards. By contrast, negative reinforcement works in a slightly different way. Desired behaviour is more likely to occur because it ensures an aversive or negative consequence is prevented or postponed. For example, if a teenager really disliked being nagged by a very persistent parent to tidy her bedroom or turn her music down at home, she is more likely to do these things in order to avoid being nagged. The parent's nagging behaviour is the negative reinforcement in this situation.

See also – Behaviourism; Conditioning; Classical conditioning; Operant conditioning; Pavlov, Ivan

Rogers, Carl

Carl Rogers (1902 – 1987) was an American psychologist who is known as one of the pioneers of humanistic psychology. This focuses on the whole person and views each person as unique, rational and self-determining. Rogers was very interested in the development of the self and made a considerable contribution to psychological understanding of human potential, the drive to grow and develop and the importance of enabling people to 'be themselves'.

Rogers (1963) was distinctive in the way he encouraged psychologists, educators and care practitioners to focus on and facilitate the capacity that people have for self-direction and for understanding their own development needs. Rogers noted that an individual's self-concept is strongly influenced by the judgements they make about themselves and by what they believe others think about them. For example, a negative self-concept can develop if a person internalises critical comments that others make about them ('you're hopeless') and then think and act as if this is true. Rogers was also concerned with the importance of self-esteem and the role of the 'ideal self' in the way that we make judgements about our selves. Humanistic psychologists such as Rogers (1963) claim that a mismatch between the ideal self and actual self can lead to psychological and emotional problems.

See also – Person-centred counselling; Self-concept; Self-esteem; Self-fulfilling prophecy

HEALTH AND SOCIAL CARE

Role / Role theory

The concept of role originated in sociology and is often referred to as a 'social role'. It refers to a set of behaviours, rights, obligations, expectations and beliefs that are associated with a particular social status and position (parent, policeman, teacher).

People perform multiple roles in their everyday life, depending on their relationship to others (as mother, father, brother, sister, grandchild etc) and their social situation (as 'employer or employee, student or professor, for example. Roles are therefore relational and also functional. Social learning theorists argues that social roles enable us to interact and behave in particular ways because we learn and 'perform' the behaviour and 'script' expected of that role (e.g as student in relation to teacher). Roles also enable a division of labour to occur in society so that some people perform the role of doctor whilst others perform social work roles or nursing roles.

See also – Bandura's theory; Role models; Social learning theory

Role models

Role models are people who inspire others to imitate or be like them because of their desirable characteristics.

Using a social learning theory approach, Bandura and Walters (1963) argued that we learn and develop through a process of imitating role models but that we also only imitate those behaviours we see as being in our interests. The idea of modelling and learning through imitation has been used to promote anti-discriminatory behaviour and to persuade people to improve their health-related behaviours. Being anti-discriminatory and promoting health and wellbeing are key features of the care practitioner's role for many people working in the health and social care sectors.

Promoting anti-discriminatory behaviour and practices
Care practitioners tend to be committed to promoting equality and challenging discrimination in their everyday work and should act as role models in this respect. Expressing anti-discrimination values in the way that they relate to and interact with people and modelling behaviours that promote equality and fairness may encourage others (colleagues and people who use services) to imitate this kind of behaviour. In this way, the social learning perspective informs the approach care practitioners take in the care relationships.

Using positive role models in health education
Role models can use the influence they have over people who aspire to be like them to shape the health behaviours of the wider public.

The concepts of role modelling, vicarious reinforcement and imitation have been widely used by health education campaigners to raise awareness of a range of health issues, including diet, exercise and breast cancer for example, in ways that encourage people to change their behaviours.

Diet, weight loss and healthy eating issues have been promoted by a range of celebrity chefs such as Jamie Oliver, Hugh Fearnley-Whittingstall and Gordon Ramsey over the past five years. Similarly, television and radio chat shows and events such as the London Marathon frequently feature celebrities who are promoting health-related causes as a way of gaining wider publicity for them whilst also encouraging fans to change their health behaviour. The use of role models like celebrities and sports performers in health education programmes is a deliberate attempt to draw on social learning principles.

See also – Humanistic psychology; Social learning theory; Role/Role theory

References
Bandura, A. and Walters R.H. (1963), *Social learning and personality development*, New York, Holt, Rinehart and Winston.

Self-actualisation

The concept of self-actualisation is used to describe the drive or motivation human beings have to fully achieve their potential and goals as a human being.

The concept of self-actualisation is commonly associated with Abraham Maslow's (1943) hierarchy of needs theory. It is the final stage, or ultimate level, of human psychological development – the actualisation of personal potential - that can only be reached when all of the individual's other basic and psychological needs have been met. Maslow's theory suggests that people have a psychological drive to achieve self-fulfillment and that a person must be making full use of their potential before they achieve this.

Carl Rogers (1902 – 1987), another humanistic psychologist, also argued that each person is born with a 'self-actualizing tendency' – that is, a need to grow and develop to his or her full potential. However, people may develop a self-concept or have expectations and demands imposed on them that do not fit with their self-actualizing tendency. Because they spend time and energy trying to conform to these expectations and demands, people in this situation will remain unfulfilled and unable to achieve their true potential.

See also – Humanistic psychology; Maslow's Hierarchy of Needs

References
Maslow, A. (1943) *Motivation and Personality*, New York, Harper and Row

HEALTH AND SOCIAL CARE

Self-concept

This refers to the idea that a person's sense of 'self' is created or constructed out of the beliefs that they hold about themselves as well as the responses others have towards them.

Self-concept is an idea developed by those using a humanistic psychological perspective. A person's self-image combines with their self-esteem to make up their self-concept. An individual's self-concept is a central part of his or her identity. Having a clear, positive picture of who you are (self-image) and how you feel about yourself (self-esteem) helps to give you a sense of psychological security and affects the way that you relate to other people.

A person's self-concept becomes more sophisticated as they progress through childhood and into adolescence and adulthood. Children move from being able to give surface, external descriptions of themselves to being able to describe their own internal qualities, beliefs and personality traits. They also become capable of making global judgements about their self-worth and self-esteem. Self-concept has an impact on a person's emotional and social development throughout the lifespan. For example, it can motivate us to do or try things (at school, at work in our personal life) or stop us from seeking or taking opportunities.

See also – Humanistic psychology; Anxiety; Self-esteem

Self-esteem

Self-esteem refers to a person's sense of their self-worth. A person's self-esteem consists of beliefs ('I am kind', 'I am useless', 'I am unlovable', 'I am beautiful') about themselves as well emotions (pride, shame, sadness, happiness) that the person feels about themselves. In essence, self-esteem is a judgement that expresses what we think and feel about our 'self'.

Psychologists generally see self-esteem as a core, enduring feature of an individual's personality and a factor that influences motivation and attainment in a person's education, work and personal life. An individual with positive or high self-esteem is, for example, thought to be more likely to be happy, achieve well and feel fulfilled in their personal life and relationships. By contrast, a person with low self-esteem is thought to be more likely to be self-critical, pessimistic and envious of others. Self-esteem plays an important part in humanistic psychology.

See also – Humanistic psychology; Maslow's Hierarchy of Needs; Self-concept

HEALTH AND SOCIAL CARE

Self-fulfilling prophecy

A self-fulfilling prophecy is a prediction, often based on false or untrue information, that comes true because of the way a person (and others) responds to it.

A self-fulfilling prophecy develops where a person's beliefs about themselves or a situation are internalised and then expressed through the way they relate to others. For example, a person may develop the (false) belief that others won't treat them with respect. The person's belief that they are not very capable, don't deserve attention or are somehow less important than others is likely to then influence the way they interact with others (being submissive, withdrawn and accepting personal criticism easily, for example). The disrespectful behaviour of others – perhaps dominating, taking advantage of or overlooking the person's needs – reinforces the negative beliefs they hold about themselves. That is, the initial prediction or prophecy based on false information comes true because of the person's own behaviour in response to it.

The phrase 'people get what they expect' captures the essence of this concept. People with high self-esteem who expect to be treated favourably because they believe they deserve to be treated well tend to generate this behaviour from other. The reverse happens to people with low self-esteem. In both cases, people's own beliefs, the way they present themselves and then behave trigger particular types of responses from others.

See also – Influence; Social learning theory; Bandura's theory

Self-harm

The concept of self-harm refers to any form of deliberate self-injury that is intentional but not suicidal.

Skin-cutting and self-poisoning are the most common forms of self-harm. Other less common forms include hair-pulling (trichotillomania), opening up cuts and wounds to prevent healing (dermatillomania), burning, scratching or hitting body parts and swallowing objects or toxic substances. There is usually a deliberate attempt to cause tissue damage in any form of self-harm. Adolescents and young adults are most likely to self-harm but self-harm does occur in all age groups.

Self-harming behaviour can be life-threatening and may have unintentionally fatal consequences. Some people do self-harm without having a diagnosed mental health problem. However, self-harm may also be a symptom of other conditions such as depression, eating disorder, post-traumatic stress disorder, anxiety disorder or borderline personality disorder.

People give a variety of reasons for self-harming. For example, for some people use self-harm as a way of coping with extreme stress, intense anxiety, depression, feelings of failure or a deep sense of self-loathing and low self-esteem. A person's self-harming behaviour may be linked to traumatic events that have happened to them – such as child abuse, sexual assault or traumatic loss – or may be linked to ongoing patterns of dysfunctional or destructive behaviour like perfectionism, addiction or self-image problems.

People who present with self-harm injuries at Accident and Emergency departments have often consumed excessive amounts of alcohol prior to self-harming.

There are a number of different forms of treatment and support for self-harm, including:

- drug treatments, especially if self-harm is linked to anxiety or depression
- teaching avoidance techniques that aim to occupy the person with other activities when they are stressed and likely to self-harm
- harm-minimisation approaches, such as needle exchanges for heroin addicts, that aim to reduce the risk involved in some self-harming behaviours
- Cognitive behavioural therapy that challenges dysfunctional thinking and destructive patterns of behaviour and equips the person with alternative ways of thinking and behaving.
- Relaxation / mindfulness techniques that aim to reduce underlying tensions and help the person to avoid stress and situations that may trigger their self-harming behaviour.

See also – Mental illness; Self-esteem; Cognitive Behavioural Therapy

Separation (and loss)

Separation anxiety refers to the distress shown by an infant or young child when separated from his or her mother and the degree of comfort and happiness when reunited.

John Bowlby (1907 – 1990), a British psychologist using a psychoanalytic perspective, believed that lasting psychological damage would be done to a child if the attachment bond between them and their mother was broken by separation. In particular, Bowlby's (1953) theory of maternal deprivation argued that separated children might grow up unable to love or care for others, might fail to achieve their educational potential and might turn to crime during adolescence and adulthood.

Psychologists working outside of the psychoanalytic tradition, such as Michael Rutter (1981), doubted that babies are so seriously harmed by separation. Rutter's evidence suggested that it is the quality of the emotional attachment between a baby / child and their carer that matters in promoting psychological development.

Separation and loss issues are a main focus of attachment theory. This is a psychological theory that attempts to explain the dynamics of short and long-term human interpersonal relationships. Separation and loss can threaten, disrupt or even rupture relationships between people in any life stage. Issues relating to separation and loss are often a feature of the work that social workers, counsellors, midwives and mental health workers do with their clients.

HEALTH AND SOCIAL CARE

See also – Early experiences; Psychoanalysis; Psychodynamic approach; Anxiety

References
Bowlby, J. (1958) *Child Care and the Growth of Love*, Harmondsworth, Penguin.
Rutter, M. (1981) *Maternal Deprivation Reassessed*, Harmondsworth, Penguin.

ABC GUIDE TO PSYCHOLOGICAL PERSPECTIVES

Stress (and coping)

In psychology, stress is a feeling of strain and pressure when faced by difficult or demanding challenges.

Small amounts of stress may be desired, beneficial, and even healthy. In fact, positive stress ('eustress') helps improve athletic and work performance. It is also a factor in motivation, adaptation, and reaction to the environment. However, health and social care workers tend to focus on the state of psychological tension caused by excessive stress ('distress') and which makes people feel they are unable to cope with everyday living and work demands. The way in which stress can be both a positive and a negative influence on health and wellbeing is described in the diagram below.

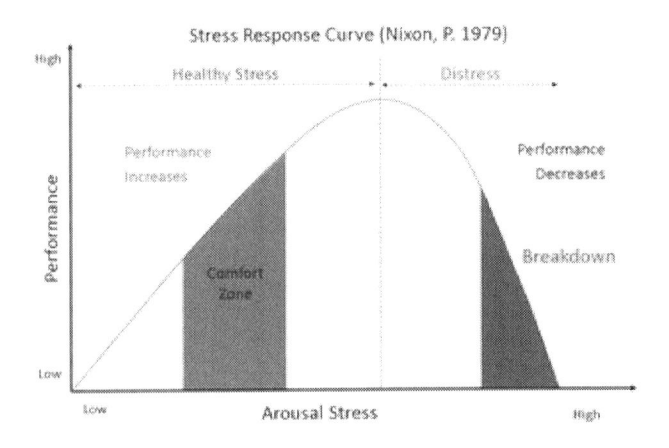

Figure 19 – The stress response curve

The notion that a person's lifestyle, work situation or personal life can have a stressful effect on them is widely held. In some situations, stress may be the consequence of personal decisions and choices. For example, some people choose to do work that is personally challenging or to work long hours to make more money. Alternatively, a combination of unavoidable factors – poor housing, debts, loss of employment, relationship breakdown, health problems - may result in a person developing a stress-related condition.

Stress can affect people in a variety of ways. Research suggests that stress experienced in infancy and childhood can have a significant effect on social and emotional development throughout life. For example, fear and uncertainty undermine the development of confidence and self-esteem. Additionally, children and adolescents who are more stressed are less likely to learn well or realise their intellectual potential.

High levels of stress in adulthood and old age can disrupt and damage a person's social relationships and have a negative effect on their self-esteem and confidence. Extreme, sudden stress as well as more low level, continuous or chronic stress is linked to a range of physical health problems, including depression, anxiety, eczema, asthma, high blood pressure, heart disease and stomach ulcers.

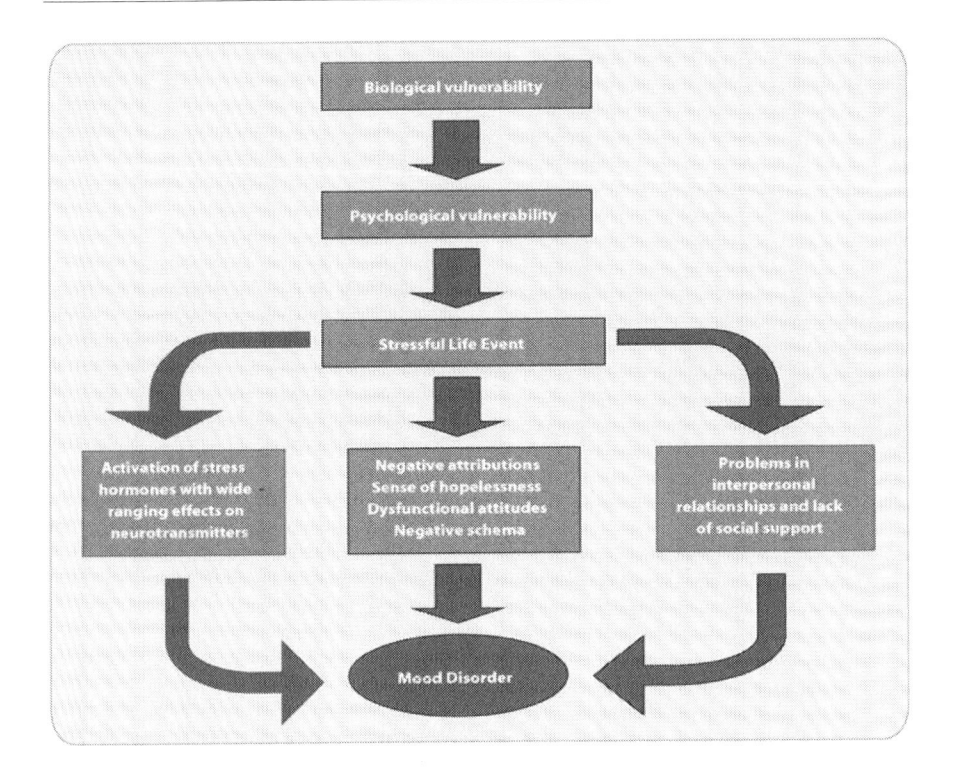

Figure 20 – An example of how the stress / vulnerability model works

Stress reduces the quality of a person's life, has a negative effect on their development and will probably lead to physical and mental health problems unless it is reduced or dealt with.

Explaining stress

Hans Selye (1907 – 1982), a Hungarian endocrinologist, provided the first scientific, biologically-based explanation of human stress reactions. Selye's General Adaptation Syndrome claimed that a stressful event that is seen as a threat to a person's wellbeing triggers a three-stage physical response:

1. **Alarm** – the body responds with a fight-or-flight reaction, activating the sympathetic nervous system. This releases hormones (cortisol and adrenalin) into the blood stream. The body responds with a fight or flight reaction until the immediate danger is over.
2. **Resistance** – the parasympathetic nervous system returns physiological functions to normal levels whilst the body keeps its resources focused against the stressor. Blood glucose, cortisol and adrenaline levels are kept high within the body. Heart rate, blood pressure and breathing rate are also elevated. The body is kept on red alert though the person may look relatively normal to others.
3. **Exhaustion** – if the stressor continues to threaten the person it will reduce and even exhaust the person's physiological resources to the point disease and the death occurs.

Selye's theory argued that the human response to stress is biologically-based and is characterised by adaptation to a perceived threat in the person's environment. Coping involves making physiological, psychological and social adjustments to avoid, manage or overcome the apparent threat.

See also – Nature versus Nurture; Biological psychology; Genetics; Nervous system; Conditioning; Personal constructs; Self-concept; Self-fulfilling prophecy

Reference
Nixon, P (1979), *The Human Function Curve*, Practitioner.

Therapy / therapeutic

A therapy is a systematic and deliberate attempt to help, change or deal with a health or psychological problem in a constructive and supportive way, usually following a diagnosis.

Medical practitioners may use the terms 'therapy' and 'treatment' to refer to the same thing e.g drug therapy (medication). Psychologists, social workers and other mental health workers tend to use the term to refer to some form of psychotherapy or counselling (a 'talking therapy') that could be used to help or empower a person to deal with emotional or mental health difficulties. There are many different forms of psychological 'talking therapy', including:

- Person-centred counselling
- Cognitive behavioural therapy
- Psychodynamic counselling
- Psychoanalysis
- Brief, solution-focused therapy
- Dialectical Behaviour Therapy (DBT)

Peplau (1988) described a therapeutic relationship as a 'human connection that heals'. Health and social care workers may develop therapeutic relationships with the people they support without being 'therapists'. This happens when an alliance is formed for a period of time between a care worker and the person in needs of care or support. The therapeutic aim of these relationships is usually related to promoting the health and well-being of the person receiving support.

See also – Psychoanalysis; Cognitive Behavioural Therapy; Person-centred counselling; Mental illness

Reference
Peplau, H (1988), *Interpersonal relations in nursing: a conceptual framework of reference for psychodynamic nursing*, New York: Springer.

Social learning theory

Social learning theory is a psychological perspective that focuses on the influence and impact that relationships and interactions with other people have on human development and behaviour.

Albert Bandura (b. 1925) is the psychologist responsible for developing some of the main principles of the social learning theory. He recognised that behaviourism could only explain how people learn directly through experience. People, and other animals, also learn *indirectly* by observing and imitating the behaviour of others. As a result, this perspective focuses on the effects that other people, such as parents, teachers, friends, peer group members, celebrities, sports performers and work place mentors, for example, can have on an individual's development and behaviour. In particular, social learning theory argues that some behaviour is acquired or learnt through imitation of admired people or role models.

The education and training of health and social care workers makes use of social learning theory in the way that learners are often paired with a mentor in the care setting and are encouraged to observe and imitate their practice. It is through observation, imitation and social interaction that trainee or novice care workers develop the attitudes and values and the professional skills and practices associated with their intended profession. Similarly, practitioners working in child care, social care, learning disability and mental health settings will often make a deliberate effort to model and demonstrate appropriate behaviour and social, interaction and coping skills.

The rationale for this, drawing on social learning theory, is that individuals who see appropriate behaviour being modelled will learn from their experiences and will then imitate it.

A range of psychological concepts that are now routinely used to understand and explain how aspects of human behaviour develops are drawn from social learning theory. Ideas such as social roles, role models and learning through observation and imitation are examples. These ideas and the general approach of social learning theory fit well with the relationship-based and interaction-focused work of many health and social care practitioners.

Evaluating social learning theory

What does it offer?	What are its limitations?
1. Social learning theory combines behaviourist with cognitive principles. This provides a powerful, practical way of promoting learning and behaviour change.	1. Social learning theory does not take into account different levels of ability or an individual's stage of intellectual development – it assumes everyone is capable of learning through observation.
2. The principles of social learning theory are simple, widely used and are seen as effective in educational settings and in care settings where teaching living skills is a feature of care practice.	2. Social learning theory does not take into account the fact that people learn through experimenting and innovating as well as by observing and imitating others – it underplays creativity
3. The outcomes of a social learning theory approach can be easily observed and are measurable.	3. Social learning theory doesn't explain how to motivate people to learn through imitation – it just suggests that this is what happens and that all people can be motivated in the right circumstances

See also – Culture; Self-fulfilling prophecy; Role theory; Role models; Bandura's theory; Group therapy; Eating disorders

Unconscious mind

Sigmund Freud (1856 – 1939), the founding father of psychoanalysis, developed a revolutionary and influential psychological theory to explain the human mind and behaviour. Part of this argued that human behaviour and thinking can be motivated by 'unconscious' processes.

Freud believed that the mind consisted of three territories:

- The conscious mind is aware of the here and now, functioning when the person is awake so that the person behaves in a rational, thoughtful way. This level or part of the mind handles all the information you receive from the outside world through your senses.
- The pre-conscious mind lies just below the surface of consciousness and contains partially forgotten ideas and feelings. It can be compared to a filing cabinet where we store everything we need to remember and which we can bring to conscious awareness easily. It also prevents disturbing unconscious memories from surfacing.
- The unconscious mind is the biggest part and acts as a store of all the memories, feelings and ideas that the individual experiences throughout life. The things that lurk deep in the unconscious are seen to play a powerful, ongoing role in influencing the person's emotions, behaviour and personality.

ABC GUIDE TO PSYCHOLOGICAL PERSPECTIVES

Freud claimed that the development and expression of a person's emotions and behaviour is driven by three interrelated structures - the Id, Ego and Superego. According to Freud, the Id and Superego are always in conflict. The Id, or unconscious part of the personality, is focused on getting what it wants. It consists of sexual, aggressive and loving instincts and wants immediate gratification. The Superego is the last part of the personality to develop as a result of socialisation. Morals and a sense of right and wrong drive it – it is the person's 'conscience'. The Ego balances the demands of the Id and Superego and is the conscious, rational part of the personality.

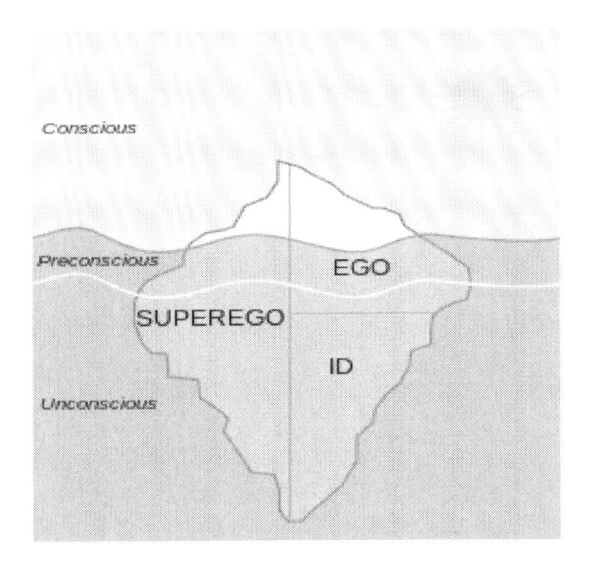

Figure 21 – The Psychoanalytic iceberg model of personality and mind

See also – Freud; Psychoanalysis; Psychodynamic perspective; Defence mechanisms

HEALTH AND SOCIAL CARE

Violence (and aggression)

Violence is 'the intentional use of physical force or power, threatened or actual, against oneself, another person, or against a group or community, which either results in or has a high likelihood of resulting in injury, death, psychological harm, maldevelopment or deprivation' (World Health Organisation). Violence is often preventable, particularly where it is triggered by excessive consumption of alcohol.

A number of different factors have been identified as a way of explaining why people sometimes use violent behaviour. These can be divided into innate, socialisation and situational factors.

Type of factor	Explanation
Innate	• Aggression and violence are seen by biological psychologists as evolutionary instincts 'hard wired' into human beings as survival mechanisms and linked to testosterone levels. • Psychoanalytical theory sees aggression and violence as an in-born tendency or drive to destroy, part of the death wish, but also linked to a survival instinct. • Neuropsychologists argue that increased aggression and violent behaviour can result from a damaged and dysfunctional brain
Socialization	• Behavioural psychologists argue that reinforcement of aggressive and violent behaviour by parents and siblings increases the likelihood of violent behaviour later in

	life. • Social learning theory suggests that observation of aggressive and violent behaviour by role models legitimates this kind of behaviour and leads to imitation.
Situational	• People living in overcrowded areas with high levels of poverty and fewer opportunities are more likely to experience and use aggression and violence in everyday life • Pain, frustration, loud noises, alcohol and hot environments are also situational factors that may combine with innate and socialised factors to trigger aggressive and violent responses • Normally non-violent people are more likely to behave aggressively and act violently when they are part of a group that behaves in a similar way.

See also – Nature versus Nurture; Social learning theory; Bandura's theory

Printed in Great Britain
by Amazon